Contemporary
SQUASH

Al Molloy, Jr.

Contemporary Books, Inc.
Chicago

Library of Congress Cataloging in Publication Data

Molloy, Al.
    Contemporary Squash.

    Includes index.
    1. Squash racquets (Game)   I.   Title.
GV1004.M64   1978   796.34'3   78-1003
ISBN 0-8092-7551-1
ISBN 0-8092-7591-0 pbk.

Illustrated by Anghelo

Published by Contemporary Books, Inc.
180 North Michigan Avenue, Chicago, Illinois 60601
Manufactured in the United States of America
Library of Congress Catalog Card Number: 78-1003
International Standard Book Number: 0-8092-7551-1 (cloth)
                                    0-8092-7591-0 (paper)

Published simultaneously in Canada by
Beaverbooks
953 Dillingham Road
Pickering, Ontario L1W 1Z7
Canada

Contents

Acknowledgments

In putting together this book on squash, I was ably assisted by a "super team" and I want to give the members of it credit for their help, suggestions and encouragement: Ed Mahan for his photography, from which drawings were made; Bruce Collins and other members of the University of Pennsylvania coaching staff for assistance with regard to information on conditioning; Susan K. Becker for writing and editing, a monumental job; and my wife, Sheila, a recent convert to squash, for her enthusiasm and typing.

Introduction

For the past 30 years, I have followed squash as both a player and a coach. I first extended my involvement in squash to a wider audience in 1963, when I wrote a manual on the game for *Sports Illustrated;* later, I participated in the production of an instructional film for the U.S. Squash Racquets Association (U.S.S.R.A.). Because participation in squash, by both women and men, has grown so dramatically in recent years and has been accompanied by significant developments in the methods of play, I think that another look at the game is in order. Squash is the ideal sport for the many people who are looking for an economical, challenging source of exercise and relaxation that they can grow with and enjoy year-round throughout their lives. It is my hope that the following guide to the pleasures and techniques of the game will serve both as an update for seasoned fans and a practical introduction for a new generation of players.

1

Genesis of the game

The game of squash originated early in the nineteenth century in the confined precincts of a debtor's prison in London, where inmates passed the time by swatting a soft ball against the walls of cell-like enclosures. The "squish" produced by the ball as it struck these surfaces gave the sport its name, an ironic heritage for a pursuit that later became associated with aristocratic schools and their alumni among the military elite, who exported the game to the British colonies. The sport took hold in the United States, where the U.S.S.R.A. was founded in 1920; it was followed eight years later by the English Squash Rackets Association.

Although squash developed almost simultaneously in America and England, the separate transformations undergone by the sport in the two countries resulted in two distinctive games, which differ with regard to size of the court, hardness of the ball, and method of scoring. The English game, now called the International game, uses a larger court, a softer ball, and a lighter racquet than the

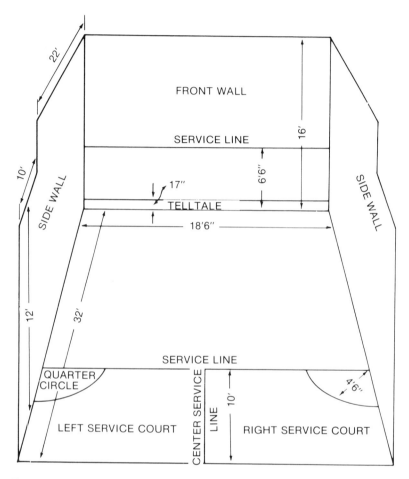

Figure 1.1. Singles court dimensions. The back-wall height is six and a half feet. The ceiling should be at least 18 feet high to allow for lights. All lines should be painted in red and should be one inch wide.

American game. Fifteen points are required to win the American game, while nine is the winning score in the International, in which a player must be serving in order to win a point and therefore must decide whether to go for the winner or play the point safely.

All these differences taken together mean that the player must develop a different strategy for each of the two games. Although the long rallies suited to the wider court

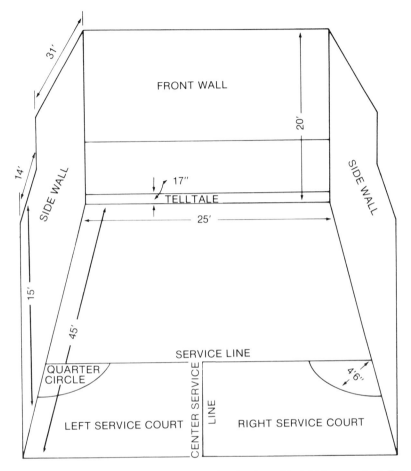

Figure 1.2. Doubles court dimensions. The back-wall height is seven feet. The ceiling should be at least 22 feet high to allow for lights. All lines should be painted in red and be one inch wide.

impose the greater physical demands, the slower game produced by the soft ball does offer certain advantages for the beginner. For example, the 70+ ball, softer than the one used previously by Americans, has tended to facilitate wrist control. The hard-ball racquet, one ounce heavier, does not rise so naturally after a shot and thus emphasizes the action of the wrist. The two racquets are discussed more fully in conjunction with selection of equipment.

2

Selection of racquet and clothing

The current variety of squash racquets is considerable as a result of two major developments: the increased popularity of the game and the American acceptance of the soft ball, which just recently was adopted by the U.S.S.R.A. for all tournament singles play. In response to this official change, I will direct my remarks to the requirements of the softer ball, with the reminder that the hard ball, still in use for doubles, requires a heavier racquet.

The basic features of the racquet to consider when making your selection are the shape and size of the grip, the weight, and the materials used in stringing.

Most racquets for the soft ball have grips that are oval in shape, but the racquets do vary in size and weight. For the beginner, I suggest a grip and racquet weight somewhere in the middle range (specific size and weight will not be marked, as they are on tennis racquets). Initially choose a racquet that feels comfortable; then, as you progress, you will no doubt be more sophisticated in your selection. For

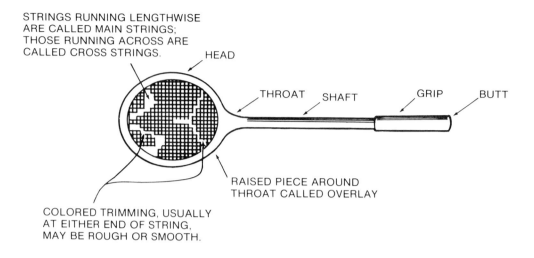

STRINGS RUNNING LENGTHWISE
ARE CALLED MAIN STRINGS;
THOSE RUNNING ACROSS ARE
CALLED CROSS STRINGS.

HEAD

THROAT   SHAFT   GRIP   BUTT

RAISED PIECE AROUND
THROAT CALLED OVERLAY

COLORED TRIMMING, USUALLY
AT EITHER END OF STRING,
MAY BE ROUGH OR SMOOTH.

Figure 2.1. Parts of the racquet (overall length 27 inches).

example, tournament players can detect variations of one-eighth ounce in racquet weight, although the entire range is only the interval between seven and a half and eight and a half ounces. Such players can also tell you whether the difference in weight is in the head or the handle. Selection of a racquet for tournament squash will depend upon the style of the individual player. Hard hitters usually favor a heavy racquet with more weight in the head, while finesse players prefer a light racquet with little weight in the head.

My final suggestion applies to all players: whatever model you choose, stay away from the bottom of the line. Such racquets may cost the least, but they also break easily and have little or no feel. Your best buy is a racquet priced in the middle of the range.

A few words must be said about the heavier racquet, which is needed for doubles and by players who still use the harder ball. This racquet comes in a variety of grip sizes and shapes usually marked A meaning oval, B meaning rectangular, and C meaning oval but quite small. For beginners, I suggest either A or B. The C grip may feel good to you in the store, but on the court it will cause you difficulty in controlling the ball. Experienced tennis players may find the B grip most comfortable

Some additional points to consider are the choice between nylon or gut in stringing, and the relative merits of toweling, as opposed to leather, on the handle. Gut is more resilient than nylon, and it consequently gives the player a little more feel for the ball and also imparts a little more zip to the ball. Although gut is unquestionably the superior material, nylon is quite satisfactory. Certainly when playing with the soft ball, the more advanced player will find a 16-gauge gut or nylon more fun to use. Remember, though, that either gut or nylon adds about one-half ounce to the weight of the racquet. Also, if nylon is your choice, be sure to use the better grades, because cheap nylon tends to be brittle and is likely to snap in a cold court. Although a press is unnecessary for a squash racquet, a cover to protect against dampness is useful, especially if your racquet is strung with gut. Either toweling or leather is fine for the handle. You may prefer toweling, which absorbs perspiration and helps to prevent the racquet from slipping in your hand. Toweling is replaced more easily and more cheaply than leather.

Your choice of clothing should be determined by considerations of physical comfort and safety. Tennis attire generally is acceptable, provided that it conforms to the regulations of your squash club, but be sure that it is loose enough to allow considerable freedom of movement. If you wear a warm-up suit to counteract a chilly court, take care to remove it before you begin to perspire. Most important, wear shoes of good quality and fit, with ample room in the toe.

3

Basic techniques

Grip

Correct grip of the racquet is extremely important, because squash is a game involving a wide variety of shots that must be made in diverse situations. A faulty grip can restrict your options and slow your progress by affecting your swing and even your footwork. The correct grip will lead to effective "racquet work," which is the ability to bring the hitting surface of the racquet into clean contact with the ball not only when it is sitting up in the middle of the court but also when it is in an awkward position. Grip the racquet correctly from the start, even though it may feel somewhat unnatural, and your progress will be speeded.

I have found the Continental grip to be the most versatile and effective grip in squash, a game of fast moves and long rallies that does not allow time to make the grip changes that are made in tennis. Most of the top-ranking players use the Continental, because it is flexible enough to

Figure 3.1. Front view of the Continental grip. The last three fingers grip the racquet; the thumb rests on the middle finger and is in a slightly diagonal position.

Figure 3.2. Back view of the Continental grip. Note slight separation of index finger from gripping fingers.

Figure 3.3. Top view of the Continental grip. The apex of the V formed by the thumb and the index finger is just to the left of center of the grip.

Figure 3.4. Side view of the Continental grip. In this illustration, notice the interplay between thumb and index finger.

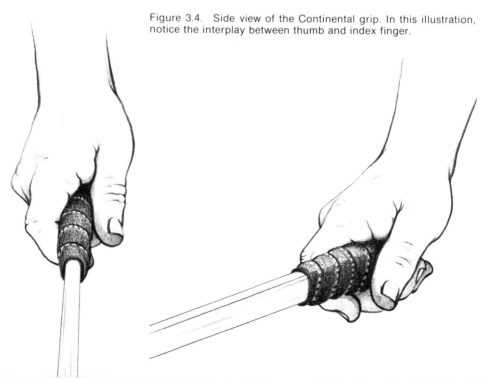

accommodate the outstretched returns called for by the extensive retrieving involved in the game, and it is ideal for playing the ball at a height between the knee and ankle, where the action in squash generally occurs.

The Continental grip will be familiar to tennis players, who are likely to use it when serving or volleying. Anyone who has never played tennis but has used a hammer will also recognize the basic features of this grip.

To obtain the Continental grip: Hold the racquet at the throat with your left hand, making sure to keep the head of the racquet perpendicular to the floor. Grasp the grip of the racquet with your playing hand; the V formed by your index finger and thumb should be just left of center and the heel of your hand should be on top of the handle. Next spread your index finger and your middle finger. Finally check that the racquet lies diagonally across your palm, and that you feel the pressure of gripping more in the last three fingers than in the palm.

Figure 3.5.   Continental grip. Racquet should lie diagonally across palm and should be gripped with the last three fingers.

Now let's analyze the grip. This method of holding the racquet frees the two sensitive fingers, the thumb and index finger, from the three gripping fingers. The resulting interplay between these two fingers, together with the placing of the thumb diagonally on the racquet, gives you racquet head control, which promotes both power and subtle responsiveness in handling the ball. Do not squeeze the grip. This causes fatigue in your hand and wrist. Just hold the racquet firmly. Make sure to reduce any tension in the forearm caused by "palming" the racquet or forgetting to spread your fingers.

The Continental grip is justifiably popular, but it does demand strong hands and wrists. For players who need to develop those areas, I suggest beginning with what is known in tennis as the Eastern forehand grip and the Eastern backhand grip, which can easily be adapted to the Continental as the player gets stronger. The Eastern forehand grip is obtained by starting with the Continental and then simply moving the heel of the hand to the right (for right-handed players). Note that the apex of the V formed by index finger and thumb is in the center of the grip. For the backhand, move the heel of the hand more on top; in this case, the V formed by finger and thumb should be well over to the left on the grip.

Figure 3.6. Incorrect grip. This would be "palming" the racquet. The index finger and thumb are sensitive fingers and should not grip the racquet as they do in this illustration.

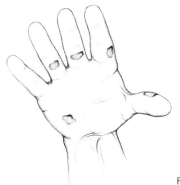

Figure 3.7. The shaded areas of the palm show where calluses may develop.

Ready position and footwork

Because squash is a rapid sport that demands constant alert anticipation and fast responses, one of your most effective tactics is to be prepared to return your opponent's shot quickly and catch him unawares. The ready position is the stance from which you can most efficiently do so. The basic position, feet straddling the center service line an inch or two in front of the service line (on the T), can be adapted to suit the energy and speed of your reflexes.

Let's look at the ready position in detail. Most importantly, try to place yourself in front of your opponent, crouching slightly, with both feet in line at a distance not greater than the width of your shoulders. Hold the racquet head up, cradling it near the top of the grip with the nonplaying hand, so that it moves with you. Keep your elbows in near the hips, back straight, and knees bent. You should feel yourself leaning slightly forward, weight on the balls of the feet, prepared to spring. Your position on the T in front of your opponent should enable you not only to move to either side but also to follow the play in back of you, a strategy essential to your safety and success.

You can easily see why mastery of the ready position is fundamental to court coverage as well as safe and swift anticipation of your opponent's shot. Correctly used, this stance will enable you to reach almost any shot in one or two steps, with enough time and area to execute your return aggressively. Such mobility also facilitates accurate reading of your opponent's intentions; you won't collide with him as you move to take his shot, or endanger him as you fire off your own.

The ability to move quickly into position behind the ball

Figure 3.8. Ready position. It is important to remember to follow the ball at all times. If your opponent is hitting the ball from either back corner, turn your head and racquet to that side and protect yourself with your racquet.

is called footwork, probably the most excessively used and least understood term in squash. You miss a shot not because of poor footwork but because of lapses in concentration that cripple your effectiveness with the racquet. Although the position of your feet is related to good footwork, the technique is most dependent upon alert positioning behind the ball.

Spin of the ball

The ball can spin in three basic ways: top spin (forward), backspin (under), and sidespin (slice). The best way to hit a squash ball is with a combination of backspin and sidespin, which provides power and control whether your intention is to hit a finesse dropshot for a nick, or to hit a blast while keeping the ball low. Although there is no great trick to achieving sidespin, it should be discussed because of its crucial role in the game.

Sidespin offers the best features of top spin and backspin while eliminating their drawbacks, such as loss of speed. If you slice the ball, which is done by drawing the racquet face across it, the resulting sidespin will retain the low bounce off the floor of top spin (forward) and the sharp downward

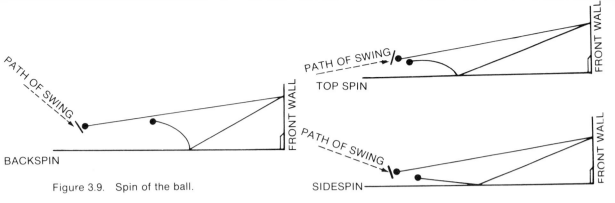

Figure 3.9. Spin of the ball.

motion off the wall of backspin (under) with no slowing of the ball. The chapter on "Ground Strokes" will describe how easily the slice can be achieved.

Watching the ball

Not too many years ago one of the tennis magazines offered $10,000 to anyone who could produce a picture of Ken Rosewall not looking at the ball while hitting it. Only one such picture was found among the millions taken of Rosewall during his remarkable career. You may have observed that Billie Jean King holds up a ball and watches it before the start of a match. And the great Hashim Khan is shown in his book holding a ball and staring directly at it. The point I'm trying to make with all these examples is that if you don't watch the ball, all your knowledge, practice, and efforts are wasted.

If you remember, I said that good footwork means getting your body behind the ball. One of the reasons why this movement is of paramount importance is that it aids you in watching the ball. If you let the ball get to your side or behind you, your head will not swivel fast enough to allow your eyes to see it. Keep the ball in front of you and watch it closely, making an effort to concentrate upon it in order to avoid being distracted by your peripheral vision, which is the cause of most missed or mishit balls. The contrast between the dark ball (generally green) and the white court will help you to focus on the ball during play.

Although watching the ball is not easy and requires work each time you play, the effort will reward you in two essential ways: it helps you to make contact with the ball in the middle of the racquet; and it stabilizes your head so that your body does not sway as you swing. These elements of the swing are crucial to maintaining power and control.

15

4

Ground strokes

At the outset, I want to dispel the idea that squash is a much more "wristy" game than tennis. Wrist control is important in both sports, but novices will use the wrist excessively, because subtle wrist action comes only with training and practice. Probably the only reason why squash has been labeled wristy is that the wrist is used to retrieve shots, and there is a good deal of retrieving per rally.

There are several key differences between squash and tennis strokes:

1. The forward swing in squash starts from above the height of the ball, to attain backspin; in tennis, it starts from below.

2. In squash, knees are bent throughout the swing, whereas in tennis they are straightened at the end in order to lift the ball over the net, for top spin.

3. In squash, the forward swing is started by the elbow; in tennis it is initiated by the shoulder, so the body seems to push forward more.

If you anticipate these differences, you will be able to switch from one game to the other and find that your reflexes will be quicker and sharper, your volley will improve, and even your confidence in hitting out on your backhand will be increased.

Let's begin with the purpose and technique of the basic strokes, which are termed ground strokes because they are hit somewhere near the top of the bounce after the ball leaves the floor and before it hits the ground again. Use ground strokes to gain control of the rally and court position by maneuvering your opponent to the front or back of the court. Hit them firmly and with "length" (see "Playing the Game"), but be alert to your opponent's position in the court, because you'll be using a full swing instead of the short swing of the volley or finesse shot.

Forehand

To develop an enduring mental image of this stroke, observe each of the following moves in a full-length mirror, starting from the ready position and proceeding as follows (assuming you are right-handed):

Figure 4.1. Start from the ready position.

Step 1. Open your racquet face by rotating your wrist as far to the right as possible, cocking it so that wrinkles appear on the top of your wrist and the back of your hand.

Step 2. Taking a small step, turn your right foot to the right side wall. Knees should be bent, with all your weight on your right foot and your left toe barely touching the ground. The fingertips of your left hand should still cradle the racquet at the top of the grip. This detail is important for the beginner, because it helps to turn the left shoulder as far to the right as possible and thus prevents the racquet arm from swinging back wildly. The racquet head should be slightly above your wrist, slightly beveled back and perpendicular to the side wall; elbows should be close to your sides, for balance and control. At this point, too, your hips and shoulders should be parallel to the side wall, with the left shoulder slightly lower, to keep your weight leaning forward toward the front wall. Quick and secure movement to this position is the key to all shots. If you are off balance at this point, you may be off balance throughout the rest of your swing.

Step 3. At this point the racquet will leave the fingertips of the left hand. Continue to turn your left shoulder as far as possible to the right, so that if you drew a straight line from

Figure 4.2. Forehand steps one and two. Rotate wrist to open racquet face. Take small step, turning right foot to right side wall.

your left shoulder, it would point to the nick at the right side wall opposite to where you are standing. The more you can swivel your hips and shoulders to the right, the better. Remember, though, that you want to turn your racquet back, not swing it. A swing might injure your opponent (who has been maneuvered to your rear), throw you off balance, and restrict your mobility in setting up to hit the ball. Turning the shoulders continues the movement of your racquet up and back, which tends to straighten your legs. Don't worry; this only helps to drive your body harder into the ball on the downswing. When you've turned the racquet back to its fullest extent, the right hand is high, close to the body for safety and control (think of a waiter holding a tray). The palm is pointing up, the wrist is cocked, and your hand is higher than your head; you are in an attitude of power similar to a pro golfer at the tee.

Step 4. Now for the left hand, which is instrumental in all shots. It aids in maintaining balance and helps to focus your eyes on the ball by reaching out as if to catch it. As the hand reaches out, the left foot steps forward to the ball, starting the downward movement of the racquet. Note that this step forward should be in the direction of the right front corner of the court, not toward the side wall. Place your left foot in the closed-stance position (note Figures 4.5, 4.6, 4.7) and you

Figure 4.3. Forehand step three. Continue to rotate hips and shoulders to the right.

Figure 4.4. Forehand step four. Reach out toward ball with left hand; left foot steps forward toward ball, starting downward movement of the racquet.

Figure 4.5.   Closed stance. It is always preferable to hit from a closed stance. The closed stance encourages more power, because it allows a longer swing. It is also preferable tactically, because it allows player to hit to all parts of the court.

Figure 4.6.   Open stance. The open stance tends to pull the ball crosscourt, thereby limiting shot selection; however, it is an effective stance when hitting volleys.

Figure 4.7.   Square stance. The square stance promotes more control but limits full power. In all cases, note that the ball is struck even with the forward foot (left foot). The right foot would be forward when hitting the backhand; in that case, the ball would be struck eight to ten inches in front of the right foot.

will achieve a fuller and stronger swing that gives the added benefit of disguising your shot. Your weight straightened out at the top of your backswing; now it is coming into full play. With the downward motion of your legs and sharp dip of your right shoulder, all your weight is behind the ball as your racquet descends to meet it. The legs not only form a strong platform to hit off but also initiate the driving force that ultimately moves the racquet head with great velocity. At this point, your wrist is still cocked and your forearm up, the right elbow close to the waist, and the racquet face still open.

Step 5. The moment of impact varies according to individual style and the direction intended for the ball. If you intend to hit the ball crosscourt, make contact earlier; if you want to hit down the line, make contact slightly later. For a benchmark, let me suggest that you try to make contact on a line opposite your left toe and at a height between your knees and ankles. In any case, try to have your right hand reach the point of impact before your racquet head, which should not drop too much below the height of your wrist. This is most important; if you uncock your wrist too soon, a mishit or loss of power will be the result. Keeping the wrist cocked until this point is not easy but can be achieved with practice. You may have overheard top players use the expression "He holds the shot well." This refers to a kind of mental pause that delays the moment of contact with the ball.

Figure 4.8. Forehand step five. Contact the ball off your left toe and at a height between your knees and ankles.

Figure 4.9. At this point you should have the feeling that you are "holding the shot."

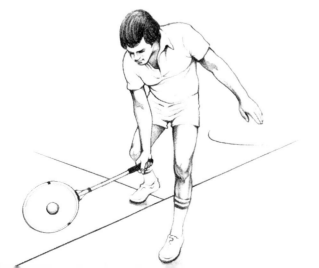

Until this point in your stroke, all the motion of your body and swing has been downward. As you may recall from the discussion of spin, we also want slice. Now it comes into play. Because of the application of so much power, there is a slight drawing of the racquet face across the ball; this results in a small amount of slice, or sidespin. Let this happen easily and naturally. All your weight should now be on your left foot, left knee still bent.

Step 6. Finish swing into left hand.

Figure 4.10.   Forehand step six. Finish the swing up into the left hand; go immediately into the ready position for the next shot.

Figure 4.11.   Finish of forehand swing with lighter (70+) ball. The racquet terminates swing up toward the left shoulder and into the left hand.

Figure 4.12.   Finish of forehand swing with heavier ball. The forearm is not pronated; the racquet head is low and the face still open. This is a good position from which to hit a finesse shot.

Figure 4.13.   Incorrect finish of forehand swing. This indicates poor racquet control and is dangerous to your opponent.

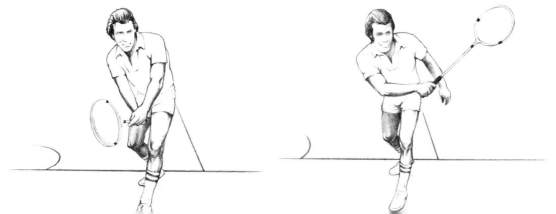

Backhand

You must develop a backhand you can rely on, for this stroke is a standby in play, used more often and with more consistent success than the forehand. It offers the easier return of shots that break in close and the greater number of potential shot openings. The ball is hit earlier than on the forehand, so you have more shot options. The reputedly difficult backhand may seem less formidable when you think of the basics of the backhand motion, which are used almost automatically in playing table tennis or dealing cards.

As we did with the forehand, let's go through the steps for the backhand and the reasons for them (assuming you are right-handed). Again, I hope you will use a mirror, to aid muscle memory.

Step 1. Using the Continental grip, which is preferable here, your first move from the ready position is to cock your wrist and turn it to the left. The back of your hand should face the ceiling and your wrist should be wrinkled. If you are using the Eastern forehand grip, you must also turn your hand a quarter turn to the left on the grip. This turn is facilitated by your left hand, which should be holding the racquet.

Figure 4.14.   Backhand. Start from the ready position.

Step 2. Free your weight by stepping toward the left side wall with your left foot. Note that this step is exactly like the one you used on the forehand. All your weight should be on the left foot, with your right toes barely touching the floor. Remember, knees should be bent, elbows should be down and close to your sides, and fingertips should be just barely cradling the racquet at the grip. The head of the racquet is above your wrist, slightly beveled back and perpendicular to the left wall. As on the forehand, you will now mentally line up the hitting surface of your racquet with the ball. With this key move, you are in position to use all the options open to you.

Figure 4.15. Backhand steps one and two. Cock your wrist and turn it to the left; step toward left side wall with left foot.

Step 3. You have decided on the drive. Continuing to cradle the racquet with your left hand, dip your right shoulder and turn it as far to the left as possible. Your racquet should not have been swung back; it should have merely turned with your body and the head should now be facing the front wall. With your right hand close to your left ear and your right elbow in close, you are in a corkscrew position, feeling as if the racquet is wrapped around your neck. Right angles are formed at your wrist and elbow, and your legs tend to straighten as you prepare to uncoil for the powerful swing.

Step 4. Step forward with your right foot. The toe of that foot should be pointed toward the left front corner as you straighten your elbow and bring the racquet forward and down to meet the ball. Maintain the cocked position of the

Figure 4.16. Backhand step three. Continuing to cradle the racquet with your left hand, dip your right shoulder and turn as far to the left as possible.

wrist and try to hit from a closed stance. Knees are bent, right hip held back somewhat. Just before impact, try to feel the mental pause.

Step 5. The point of impact is approximately eight to ten inches in front of the right foot. For power and control, be sure that your racquet hand precedes the racquet head to the point of contact with the ball. The release of so much accumulated force will impart slice to the ball, but again, as in the forehand, be sure to maintain your balance and control of the racquet. It should now be angled back and pointing toward the front wall, with the head higher than your wrist. Your shot is delivered with all your weight on the bent right knee; the left toe is pivoted forward, just touching the floor.

Step 6. Finish of swing.

Figure 4.17. Backhand step four. Step onto right foot, toe pointing to left front corner as you straighten elbow and bring racquet forward and down to meet the ball.

Figure 4.18. At this point, you should have the feeling that you are "holding the shot."

Figure 4.19 (left).   Backhand step five. Contact the ball eight to ten inches in front of right foot. Figure 4.20 (center). Backhand step six. Finish the swing. Figure 4.21 (right). Finish of backhand swing with the lighter (70+) ball. The racquet is up, ready for the next shot.

Figure 4.22 (left). Finish of backhand swing with the heavier ball. Note that the wrist has straightened. This makes recovery for the next shot difficult, but is, however, a good position for a finesse shot. Figure 4.23 (right). Incorrect finish of backhand swing. This indicates poor racquet control and is dangerous to your opponent.

5

Serve and return of serve

Although the serve and return of serve in squash look less formal and rigid than they do in tennis, they actually involve a good deal of skill and planning. The three basic serves are the lob, the slice, and the hard serve. Your choice will depend upon such factors as the temperature of the court and ball, the tempo of play, your condition and that of your opponent, and the score. Below are tips on executing and returning the serve. For complete details on technical matters, see "Singles Playing Rules."

Serve

Lob serve

The lob is the standard serve for players at all levels. It is easy to execute and, if done well, it is difficult for the opponent to return successfully, much less aggressively. Assuming that you are right-handed, start with the right foot completely within the lines of the quarter circle. The correct starting position for all three serves is the first stage of the position for hitting a forehand drive, except that you are holding the ball in your left hand, which also cradles the raised racquet head. Your right foot is parallel to the front wall, knees are bent, and the left foot is ready to stride forward.

After checking to see if your opponent is ready and where he is standing to receive, take the racquet back lower than the height of the ball, to a position approximately parallel with the side wall. The racquet face should be open, the movement of the racquet head controlled. Extend your left hand forward and stride toward the front wall with your left foot while bringing your racquet forward. The whole motion should feel as if you are lifting the ball up as high on the front wall as possible, without hitting it. To accomplish this, your knees will straighten out and your finish will be high, racquet pointing to the top of the court. Because of the low-to-high action, the ball will get a slight amount of top spin. This is good, because top spin gives a little more loft to the ball when it hits the front wall, which is an advantage on high-ceilinged courts. Remember, this is a lob serve and not a hit; your intent is to get the ball up as high and as softly as you can with almost zero speed. Your opponent is then confronted with the dual difficulty of hitting and forcefully returning a high ball that offers little resistance to his racquet. After you have served, quickly continue forward off your left foot to the T, so that you will maintain the advantage of firing an aggressive shot off a weak return.

Now that you know the mechanics of hitting the lob serve, the question is where to aim it. The best spot on the front wall varies from court to court and within each match as the ball gets warm; to adjust to this, you must know where the rebound off the front is to go. Aim for the side wall of the receiver's court *behind* the quarter circle and six to eight feet up. Although you can hit a service ball on the bounce, you should learn to hit it out of your hand, because this method gives you more control.

Hard serve

The increasing popularity of the hard serve has affected the nature of the game, because it definitely gives the server greater options (see Figure 5.5).

Begin with the basic starting position and then, instead of taking the racquet head back low, bring both hands up. Toss the ball forward and up and draw the racquet back behind the head with the elbow high, like a quarterback ready to release a pass. Now stride forward onto your left foot and swing forward and somewhat down on the ball. Aim to hit close to the service line without hitting the line, so that the ball starts down off the front wall. Although it can be risky, the hard serve is a great way to keep your opponent off balance by harassing him from a variety of angles. Remember that on most hard serves, the ball should first hit the back wall, not the floor, where it tends to sit up.

Slice serve

The whole motion resembles the hard serve, except that the ball is thrown more to your right side, no higher than your head. As you step forward with your left foot, the action of your racquet is down and across the ball: an outside-in swing. This serve is hit close to the service line and intended to strike your opponent's side wall near the service line at varying heights (see Figure 5.12).

Return of serve

The rule "Always face the nearest side wall" is essential when returning serve. Taking the ready position, turn toward the wall nearest you. You should be approximately three feet from the back wall, with your heels on the center service line. All serves, except those that break sharply across the T, should be returned with your backhand, if that is the court you are receiving in, and with the forehand, if you are receiving in the forehand court. As the receiver, you

33

Figure 5.1 (left). Lob serve. Start with right foot completely within the quarter circle, parallel to the front wall. Figure 5.2 (center). Extend your left hand forward and stride toward the front wall with left foot while bringing racquet forward. Figure 5.3 (right). Finish high, with racquet pointing to the top of the court.

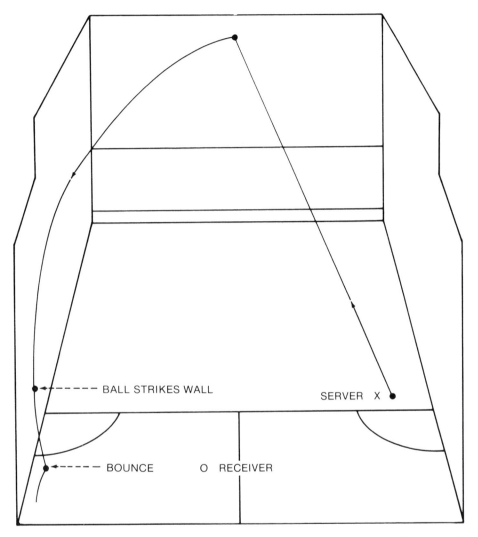

BALL STRIKES WALL

SERVER X

BOUNCE   O RECEIVER

Figure 5.4.   It is best to use the forehand from either the right or the left court. Try to have the ball hit high on your opponent's side wall and die going to the back wall.

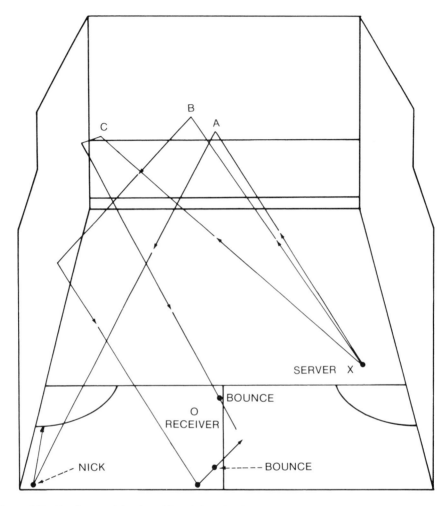

Figure 5.5. Hard serve A is played for nick on back wall; at worst, it should hit back wall on the fly and run down the side wall. A variation would be to aim it to hit opponent off the front wall as he waits to receive. Hard serve B must be hit higher on front wall so that it breaks fast and jams the receiver. Hard serve C breaks fast in front of the receiver; this is more of a trick shot.

Figure 5.6 (left).   Hard serve. Toss the ball forward and up and draw the racquet back behind the head with elbow high. Figure 5.7 (center). Stride forward on left foot and swing forward and down on the ball. Figure 5.8 (right). Aim to hit close to the service line so that the ball comes down off the front wall.

Figure 5.9 (far left). Slice serve. The motion resembles the hard serve, except the ball is tossed to the right no higher than the head. Figure 5.10 (center). The action of the racquet is down and across the ball. Figure 5.11 (left). An outside-in swing.

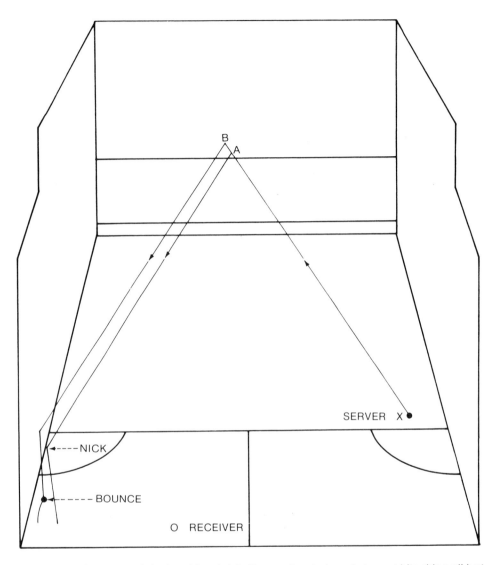

Figure 5.12. Slice serve A is aimed for nick in the quarter circle and at worst hits side wall just above floor, so that it breaks down and away from opponent. It must not come off back wall. Slice serve B is a variation of A and is used when you feel your opponent is coming forward fast in anticipation of volleying slice serve A. This would jam him with a ball at shoulder height. It must not come off back wall.

are in a defensive position, so your aims are to get the ball back and to move your opponent out of the T. The best way to do this is by volleying. The only exception to this rule is when your opponent makes a poor serve that strikes the side wall and comes off the back wall. In that case get ready, take your time, and keep the ball on your left side for a forehand and your right for a backhand. Remember, *all* other serves should be volleyed, ideally *before* they hit the side wall.

Taking the serves in order, here are your possible responses:

Return of lob serve

The percentage return is to lob down-the-line. Try to volley the ball before it hits the wall, or, if necessary, just after. Above all, don't let the ball drop too low. Try to keep your lob as close to the side wall as possible and have the ball bounce in the quarter circle. Allow your opponent to move in front of you as he goes to the back wall and you move smoothly to the T.

Return of hard serve

Return this serve cross-court, because when your opponent serves hard, he is leaning toward the T and momentarily off-balance, and a cross-court shot could get behind him. Don't attempt to return down-the-line until you are confident you can handle the speed involved. Also, don't try to hit the ball low, and be prepared to volley into your court the ball that breaks sharply across the T.

Return of slice serve

Again, return cross-court and volley. This might be called the "sucker serve," because the server's intent is to make you move forward quickly to volley and then to catch

Figure 5.13. Forehand return of lob serve. Having moved from a waiting position on the center service line, try to volley the ball just before or immediately after the ball has hit the side wall, but not while it's on the wall.

you with a ball up high, or to have you stay back and catch the nick in the quarter circle.

Your main objective in returning serve is to get the ball into play and exchange positions with the server. Take all possible opportunities to hit from close to the T and try to back up on a poor serve instead of turning on it.

Figure 5.14. Backhand return of lob serve. Try to keep your lob as close to the side wall as possible and have the ball bounce in the quarter circle.

6
Volley

The volley is crucial. Without it, you will have to cover more court than your opponent; with an effective volley, however, you can run your opponent in hopes of getting a weak return that sets the ball up for your ground stroke. If you "think volley," you will anticipate your opponent and gain control of the game with a bombardment of astutely chosen shots. The volley is not difficult, because the ball is taken in the air before it bounces, thereby using the pace of your opponent's shot against him. The essentials for a good volley are mental and physical alertness and a good ready position.

Forehand volley

Your first move is the same as that for the forehand ground stroke: open the face of your racquet. I might add that the Continental grip is much more effective than the Eastern here. Next (if you are a right-hander), turn your

45

Figure 6.1 (left). Forehand volley. Start from the ready position. Figure 6.2 (right). Open the face of your racquet and turn your right foot toward right side wall, keeping shoulders and hips open.

right foot toward the right side wall, keeping your shoulders and hips open. At this point, your left hand is still cradling the racquet and the racquet head is up. Line the ball up with the racquet face and step to it; that's all.

Your point of contact with the ball tends to send it crosscourt. Beginners should leave down-the-line volleys to advanced players and avoid hitting volleys that are higher than the shoulders. You'll have plenty of time to take most of these off the back wall. Because you are hitting the ball

Figure 6.3 (left). Line the ball up with the racquet face and step to it. Figure 6.4 (right). Very little swing is used and little wrist is needed. The finish leaves you in a strong position for the next volley.

below shoulder height, the racquet head will come down to meet the ball, putting underspin on it. Because you made contact forward of where you hit the ground stroke, the racquet tends to come slightly across the ball too and put slice on it. Very little swing is used, and little wrist is needed: the whole motion is a punch. Note that the finish of the shot leaves you in a strong position for the next volley. Finally, because you use the volley to rush your opponent, aim your shot for length to the back of the court.

Figure 6.5 (left). Backhand volley. Start from the ready position. Figure 6.6 (right). The first step is to bevel the racquet face; then step slightly to the left.

Backhand volley

The only difference here is that you execute it from the left side. Again, step one is to bevel the racquet face. Next, free your weight by stepping slightly to the left, racquet still cradled in your left hand. Sight the ball, then step in with your right foot and punch the ball crosscourt.

Figure 6.7 (left).   Sight the ball; then step in with right foot and punch it. Figure 6.8 (right). Aim your shot for length to the back of the court.

7

Auxiliary shots

Muscle memory is essential if you are to capitalize on the limited time available to put your carefully learned strokes into action during a game. A mirror is a big help; you can also use a wall in the court. Stand with your back to the wall, heels about eight inches from the wall and feet spread the width of your shoulders. You should be in a somewhat sitting position: knees bent, buttocks touching the wall. Now go through your swing: if you touch the wall with the racquet, your swing is out of control and would endanger your opponent.

For the beginner who wants to practice hitting the ball by himself, I have included the following drills, which condition the body to the length of the racquet and hit of the ball.

Forehand

Stand on the right quarter circle facing the side wall, approximately four feet away from it, with feet about one

Figure 7.1 (left). Forehand practice. Take racquet back with wrist cocked, elbow at side and racquet face beveled open. Figure 7.2 (right). Toss ball gently to side wall so that it rebounds near service line; stride forward with your left foot.

foot apart. Take your racquet back parallel to the ground and the side wall. Your wrist is cocked up and back, your right elbow is into your side, your knees are bent, and the racquet face is beveled open. With your left hand, toss the ball gently forward onto the side wall, ideally so that it rebounds from the wall to the floor near the service line. Stride forward with your left foot, left toe pointing to right front corner, and bring your racquet forward. Make contact with the ball at a point opposite your left toe and finish into your left hand. Pause and check what you have done, then go over it again until you feel comfortable. First practice your swing, then work on controlling the ball.

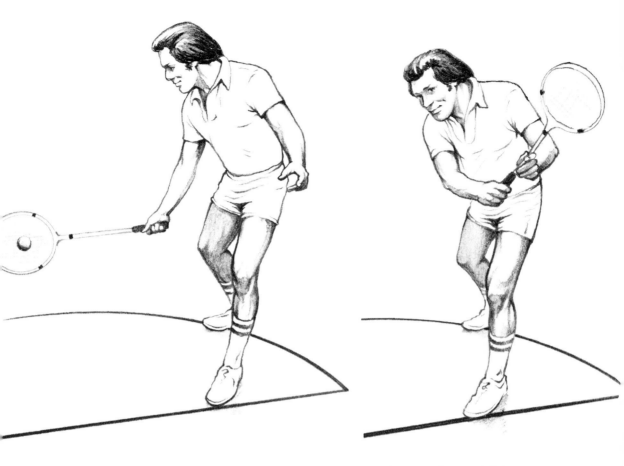

Figure 7.3 (left). Bring racquet forward and contact ball at a point opposite your left toe.
Figure 7.4 (right). Finish swing, bringing racquet to your left hand.

Backhand

Now go to the backhand quarter circle and repeat, starting from the same crouched position. Feet are about one foot apart, racquet is parallel to the wall and ground, its hitting surface slightly beveled back. Hold the ball in the fingertips of your left hand and toss it forward to the side wall so that you contact it about eight to ten inches in front of your right foot. To make this toss, your left hand will be under the racquet near the grip: this allows your left hand to come back and hold the racquet again before hitting the ball.

A few words for beginners: don't be overanxious to hit

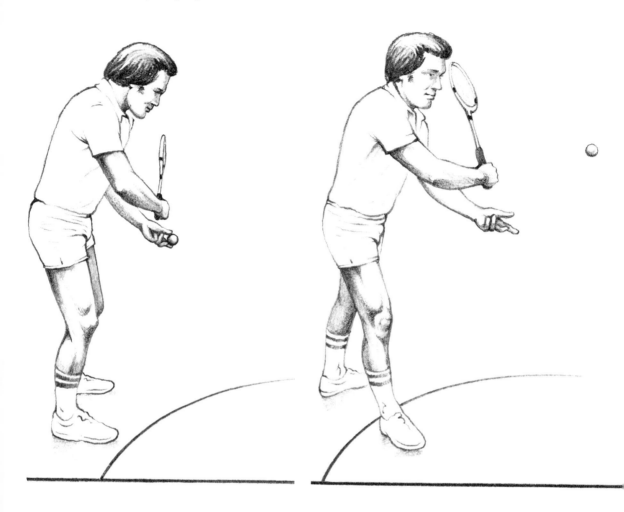

Figure 7.5 (left). Backhand practice. Stand with feet one foot apart, racquet back parallel to wall and ground. Figure 7.6 (right). With your left hand toss the ball to the side wall; left hand will be under the racquet near the grip.

Figure 7.7 (left). Contact the ball eight to ten inches in front of your right foot. Figure 7.8 (right). Finish the swing.

Figure 7.9 (left). Playing the shot close to back wall. When playing the ball in the back corners of the court, either forehand or backhand, turn more toward the back wall. Figure 7.10 (right). Poor position for taking the ball in the back of the court. Player cannot get a full swing at the ball.

the ball. Following are a few additional facts useful to both beginners and advanced players:

1. You don't always have to chase the ball. On the contrary: if the ball hits the wall, you must get away from it.
2. When hitting, always face the nearest wall. Any ball to the right of the center service line is a forehand; any ball to the left is a backhand. The closer you go to the back wall, the more you must turn to face it.

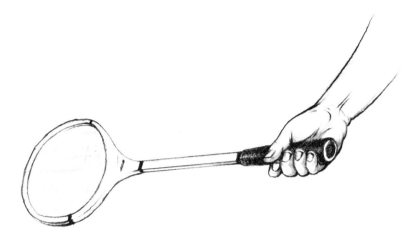

Figure 7.11 (above). Playing close-to-wall shot. Correct angle of racquet face when playing a ball close to the wall. Figure 7.12 (below). Incorrect position of racquet face when the ball is near the wall. You may not get the ball back and are likely to break your racquet.

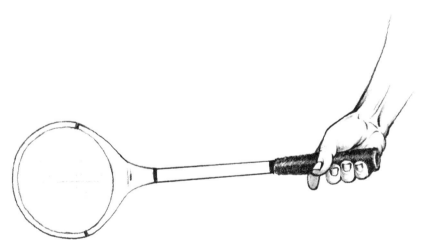

3. Although balls immediately in front of you present little difficulty, I recommend that beginners hit them crosscourt, not down the line.

4. It is not recommended to hit the ball into the back wall in order to return it. If you must do so, be sure to direct it crosscourt, away from you.

5. In order to return a ball that is close to the wall or floor without breaking your racquet, bevel the racquet face back (the racquet face will be open).

8
Practice

Squash is easier to practice than almost any other game, because all you need are a court, a ball, a racquet—*and* a clearly defined goal. If you go into the court with no organization or expectations, you will become bored and will accomplish very little. In fact, you may even ruin whatever skills you have. Five areas considered essential are skills, physical condition, mental condition, experience, and tactics. All five can be covered daily while you work out alone; you can even create tactical problems and practice the optimum shot for each. The best regimen is a mix of solo practice and competitive play: time in the court alone to work out flaws in your game and practice with an opponent to see if you have overcome them.

After you have done some stretching exercises, warm up the ball by hitting forehands and then backhands to yourself from behind the service line. These shots should be hit with a full stroke but with less than full power, and they should strike high above the telltale, for length. Your objective is to warm up both yourself and the ball while getting a feeling of consistency. Next, move nearer to the forehand and backhand side walls in turn, again working on length. Now you are ready to work on the drills that suit your individual needs. A number of useful practice drills are diagramed on the pages that follow.

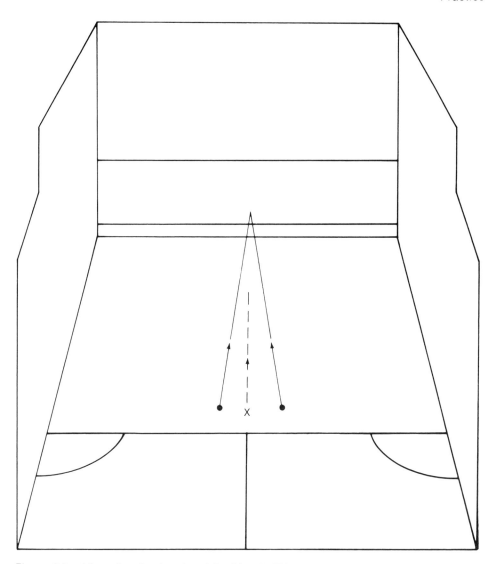

Figure 8.1. Alternating forehand and backhand. This drill can be done with both ground strokes and volley. Start on the service line and gradually work your way forward to the front wall. Because you are working on quickness you will face the front wall, but try to turn the shoulders.

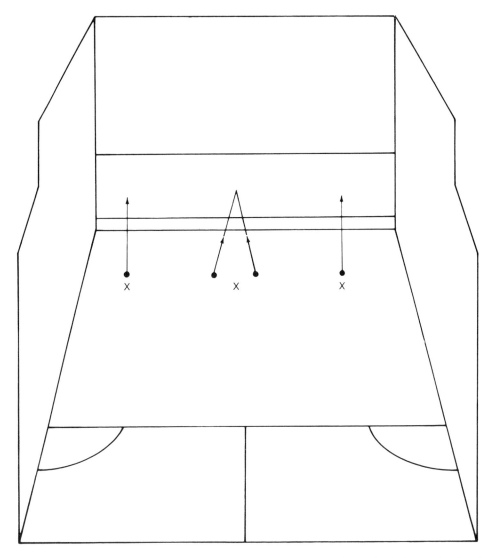

Figure 8.2. Volley. Practice volley from either side of the court, alternating between forehand and backhand. See how long you can keep the ball in play. Great for ball control.

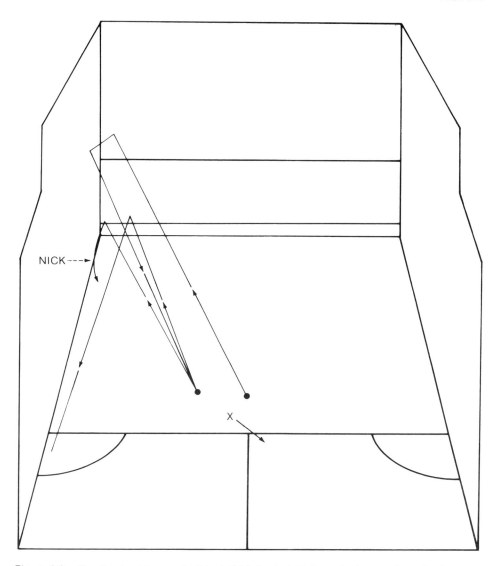

Figure 8.3. Practice backing up. In this drill hit the ball high on the front wall, so that it breaks out into the middle of the court. Then step back, imagining your opponent behind you (you are backing him up). Then step forward and hit ball down the line for length. When you become proficient, you can also play it for a dropshot nick. Practice this on both sides of the court.

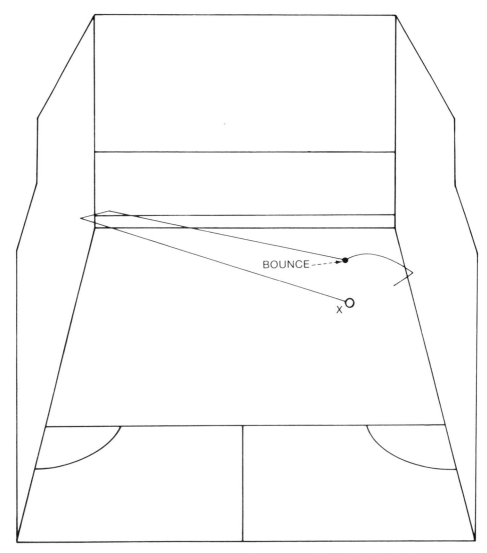

BOUNCE

X

Figure 8.4. The reverse corner. This shot can be practiced from both the forehand and the backhand sides of the court. The object is to keep the ball going and feel the width of the court. Don't worry about how low you hit the ball or whether you take it off the side wall on the second bounce. Just keep it going, much like a boxer on a light bag.

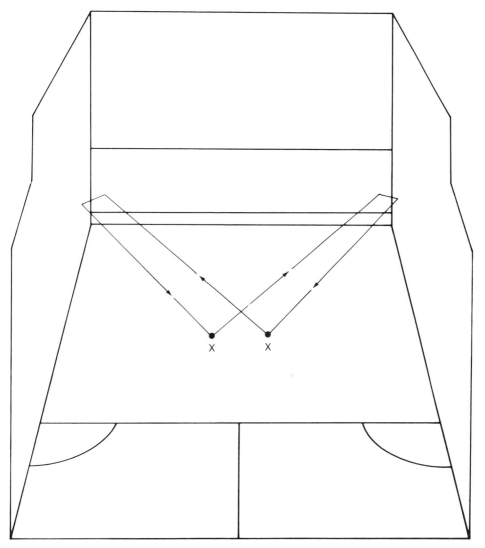

Figure 8.5. Around the corners. This is an excellent drill for developing both ball control and fast footwork. It is important to move your feet to hit either forehand or backhand. The height above the telltale can be varied, and even volleys can be practiced in this fashion. The volley, however, does take some advanced skill.

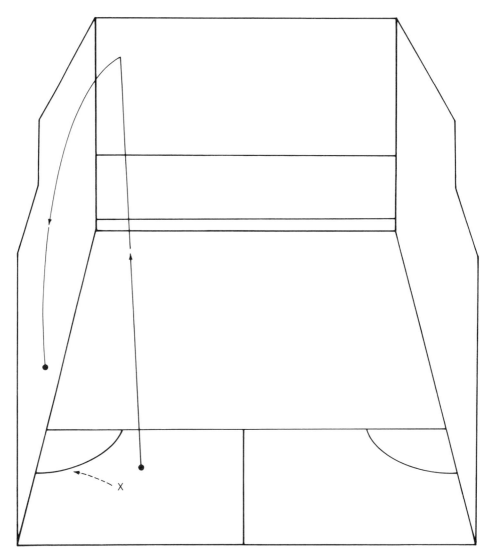

Figure 8.6. Practice returning lob serve. Lob the ball up to yourself first, returning it as a down-the-line lob. Then try variations such as a down-the-line drive, a reverse corner, a crosscourt drop, and a hard crosscourt for length.

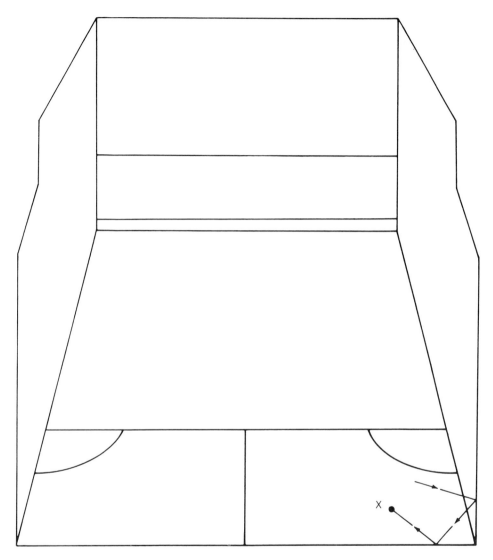

X

Figure 8.7. Back-wall practice. Throw the ball into the side wall so that it caroms off the back wall, then hit a drive for length. Important: On the forehand side, make sure that you turn toward the back wall as the ball comes off it and position yourself so that the ball is on your left side; for the backhand court, the ball should be on your right.

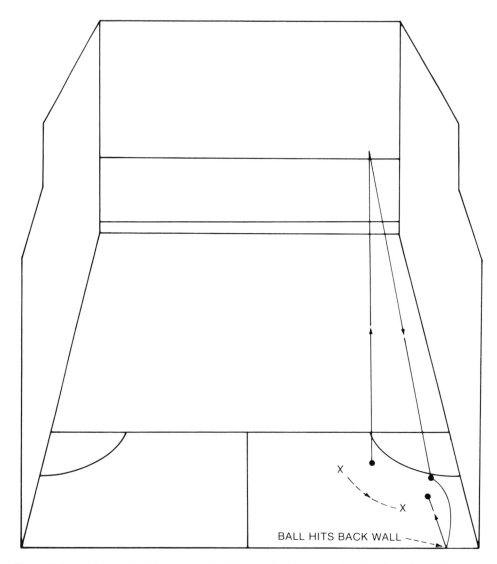

Figure 8.8. Taking ball off the back wall. Hit the ball high on the front wall so that it bounces going to the back wall. Move back to retrieve it, remembering to follow the ball with your racquet all the way. Then drive it down the line or crosscourt. Variation: Hit it to the front wall so that it hits the back wall before the floor, then bounces on the floor before you hit it.

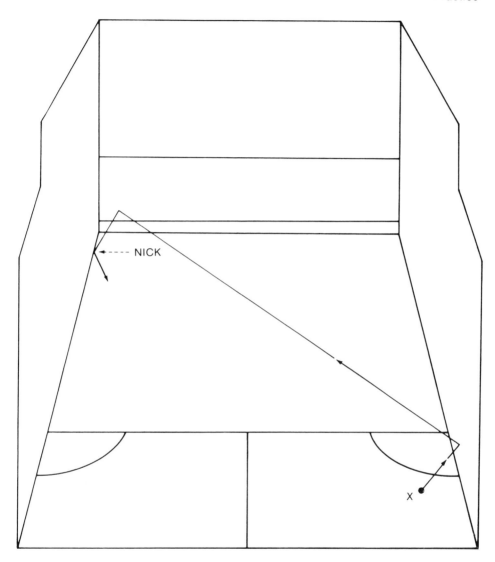

Figure 8.9.   Boast shot. Great for getting the feel of the court and developing accuracy. Hit the ball out of your hand hard into the side wall and aim for nick on the opposite side wall. The ball will roll back to you. Pick it up and do it again. Top players will get nine out of ten dead nicks with this drill. Do from both sides. Remember to turn well around toward the wall.

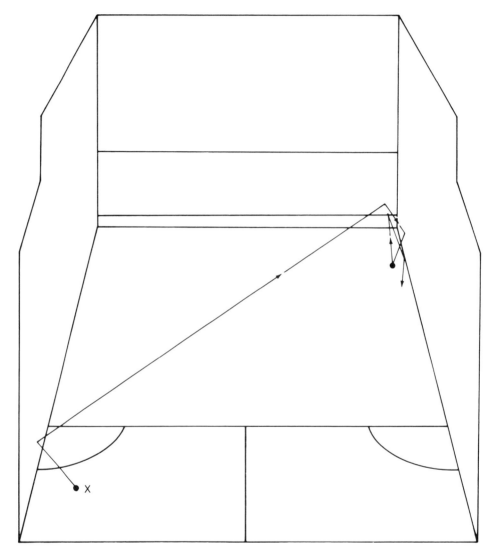

Figure 8.10. Boast shot variation. This time play your boast and then run up and play a dropshot for a nick. You'll have to be quick.

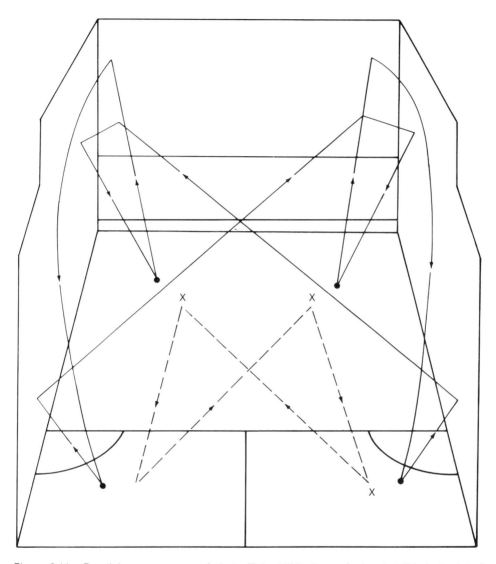

Figure 8.11. Practicing a sequence of shots. This drill looks confusing, but it is just a lot of running. Start by hitting a high boast. Then run up to the front of the court and lob the ball down the line, chase it to the back of the court, and boast again. Repeat to other side of the court. See how long you can keep it going.

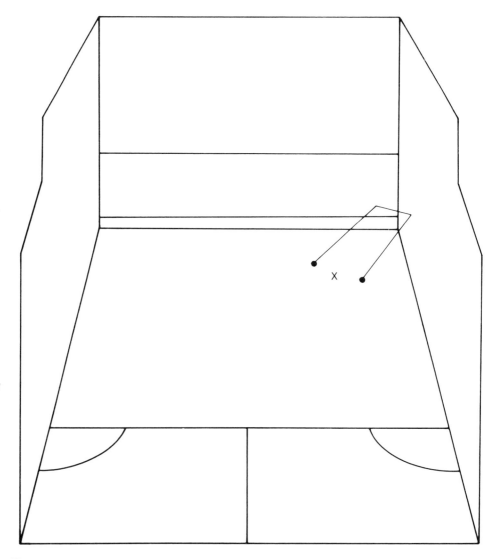

Figure 8.12. Touch shots. No practice is ever complete without practicing touch shots up front. The ball must be warm, however. Remember to stay low and try to slice the ball more than usual. Great for ball control. Do on both sides of court.

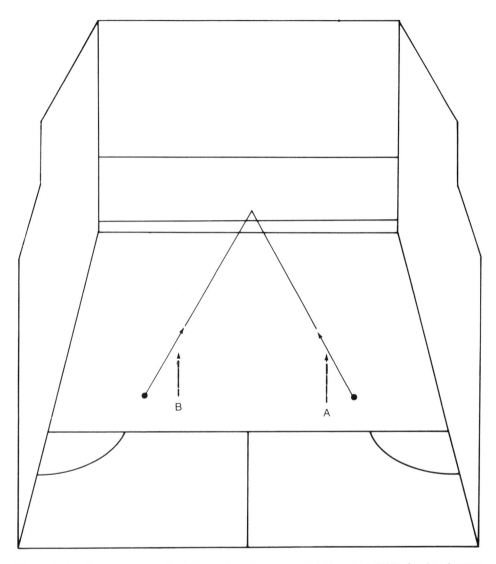

Figure 8.13. Crosscourt practice. (Assuming players are right-handed) A hits forehand cross-court; B hits backhand. As control and proficiency develop, gradually move forward. Helps to develop reflexes and ball control.

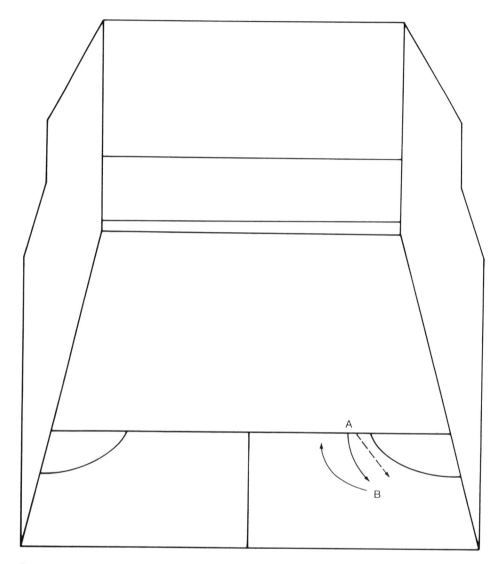

Figure 8.14. Practice hitting for length with partner. B starts by hitting a high drive down the line; ball should bounce in quarter circle. Note that A does not back along dotted line, but swings out slightly. B must give room to A. A then hits drive for length and repeats. Do the same on the backhand side.

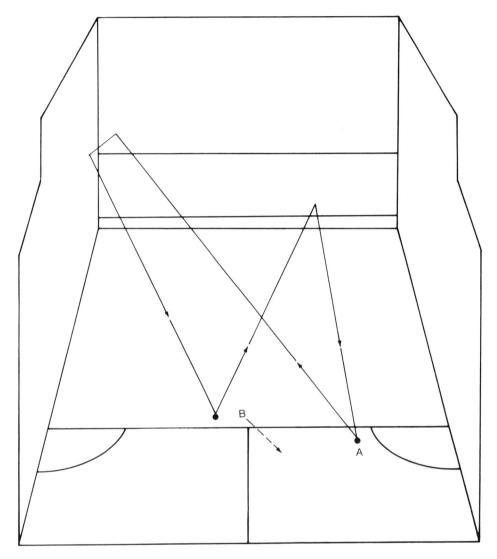

Figure 8.15. Backing-up practice. A sets up the ball by hitting it high on the front wall, breaking it off side wall. B prepares (as in diagram) to hit backhand and moves back to take advantage of A's poor shot. B should be facing left wall, with right leg well back, but ready to step forward on it to hit. B should be cognizant of openings, but should hit back to A to repeat the sequence. Do on both sides.

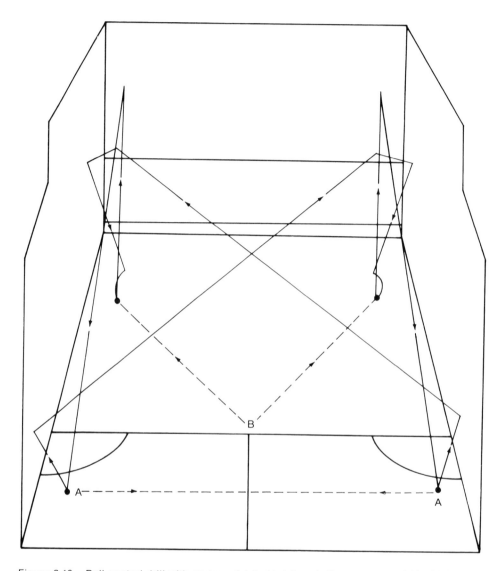

Figure 8.16.   Ball control drill with partner. A hits high boast; B moves up and hits high length shot down the line. A moves over and again hits high boast. Repeat as long as possible. Great for ball control and conditioning. Switch positions. (As diagramed, B would, in all probability, hit a straight drop for a nick, so be aware of this possibility.)

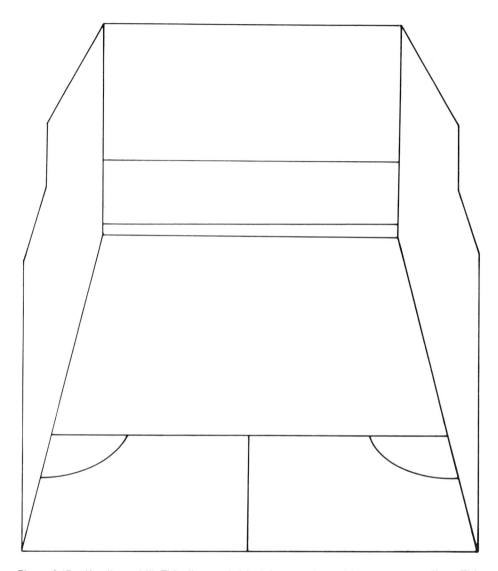

Figure 8.17.   Kamikaze drill. This diagram is blank because it would have too many lines. This drill needs a third person to keep time. The object is to play the ball for one solid minute with an opponent, then rest 30 seconds and repeat as often as possible. The ball is always in play, and two and even three bounces count, but be careful. A great conditioner.

9

Playing the game

With every shot you play in squash, you must keep two things uppermost in your mind: to execute the shot well without endangering your opponent and to give your opponent a fair opportunity to retrieve it. Remember, you are in close proximity to your opponent, playing with a lethal weapon and without protective equipment; therefore, your competition must be tempered with mutual respect. The rules of the game are written to cover this point, but any rule can be circumvented if a player does not intend to abide by its spirit. On the other hand, a champion player loves the challenge of encouraging and even mentally assisting his opponent to retrieve his best shot. A top player's concentration is totally focused upon the match, win or lose.

To achieve this level of performance, you must practice, know the limits of your skill, and read and fully understand the rules. Then you are ready to appreciate your opponent's skills and limitations and to put your own knowledge to work. This chapter is a discussion of tactics. Before analyzing them, however, I want to define the rights of each player in the court. Simply stated, these are: (1) if you intend to strike the ball from behind your opponent, go behind him to the middle of the court; (2) if you strike the ball in front of him, move forward to the middle, (3) if you are even or on a parallel line with him, hit it away from yourself. Follow these rules, and you will give your opponent free access to the ball (to which he is entitled) and cause few, if any, infractions of them. Let's play.

The position in the court most sought after is the T, because from here play can best be directed. This is not to say that you cannot win the point from another position, but if you hold the T, you will have more opportunities to fire a winning shot and, if necessary, to retrieve your opponent's good shots. Although reaching the T should be foremost in your mind, don't make this goal so all consuming that you find yourself dashing madly there, only to find the ball going off in some other direction. Instead move smoothly to the T while following the ball in anticipation of your opponent's next shot. By all means, get to the T quickly, but maintain your balance and control.

Keep in mind that there are three separate parts to every rally: (1) retrieving, (2) the put-away, (3) jockeying for position. Let's take them one at a time.

Retrieving

You should feel that every ball can be returned; in fact, all but a few "dead nicks" can. Never quit on the ball and you'll be surprised by how many you can get. In squash, unlike tennis, you have the walls to contain the ball, so hardly any setup can be considered a definitive or nonreturnable shot.

The put-away

Here again, no shot in squash is definitive. When you have an opening, take your time and don't hit the tin,

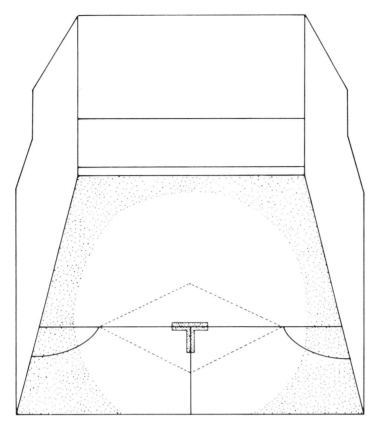

Figure 9.1. Tom Byrne, one of the top squash professionals, now retired from the New York Athletic Club, considered the T position to encompass a diamond-shaped area as illustrated. The thought was to keep your opponent from hitting from or through this area. Your shots should be designed to force your opponent to hit from the perimeter of the court (in shaded area).

because this could cost you the point. Treat the put-away as nine-tenths of a point; that is, get your opponent as far away from the middle of the court as possible and pass him while he is out of position. Again, avoid making the hurried error.

Jockeying for position

The vast majority of shots are those when neither player has clear-cut control of the play. In this case, play for length and try to design your shots so that you can get control of the play and the middle of the court. Too often in this situation, a player shoots for a winner one or two shots earlier than he should. Remember: one great shot does not win a match.

The following list of tips may be useful to you when planning the strategy and tactics you may want to use against an opponent:

1. Try to hold the middle of the court.

2. Stay in a crouched position always, with the racquet head up and your weight slightly forward.

3. Always follow the ball. If you are in the middle, turn your head slightly and watch the ball behind you.

4. As soon as you detect where the ball is going, align racquet to ball, cock your wrist, and open the face of your racquet.

5. Stay close enough to the ball to conceal the direction of your shot, but far enough away to have a free swing.

6. Try to delay the hit.

7. Hit across face of the ball.

8. Always try to hit while facing the nearest wall.

9. When hitting the ball off the back wall, turn at least 45 degrees toward the back corner and stay low.

10. Use three basic shots: alley, crosscourt, corner. Vary the speed of these shots; e.g., an alley shot can be a dropshot.

11. When behind your opponent, use the high alley (sometimes a lob) or crosscourt.

12. In front of the T position use the alley or corner.

13. If your opponent crowds you, hit crosscourt. Do not try to hit your opponent, but play the ball close to his knees. He has a blind spot there.

14. Use a corner shot when your opponent is behind you, playing the ball to the wall he is nearest.

15. Generally do not play a corner shot off a corner shot. If you must, play the same corner your opponent has just played.

16. Do not try to outslug a slugger; slow his pace down with a lob.

17. If your opponent is slow, move the ball quickly down the line and play corner shots.

18. Do not try to kill every ball; wait for the opening. Keep the ball between six inches and one foot over the tin; when hitting down the line, keep it six

inches to one foot from the side wall. Give yourself a margin for error.

19. Be careful not to underplay; for example, do not take your opponent for granted.
20. Volley whenever possible, but do not volley a ball shoulder high or above, unless it is a return of lob serve.
21. Find and play your opponent's weakness.
22. Never change a winning game.
23. Do not aim for the tin unless the ball is around knee height.
24. Return serve high down the line and move to the T.
25. Occasionally hit a low return of serve crosscourt.
26. Take a chance when you are three points ahead.
27. Tighten up your game and wait for openings when the score is around eight all.

Squash is a three-dimensional game, but too many players fail to take advantage of the full space of the court. They tend to play a couple of inches above the telltale and too close to the side wall, but rarely if ever, attempt to hit up high except to use the lob serve. Try to win all points, remembering that matches are won on few errors, not on great shots alone.

Length

All things being equal, if you are to carry one thought in your mind when going into a match, that thought should be "length." Put simply, length is the ability to direct the ball to the back of the court. Playing the ball for length is no easy matter, however; it requires skill equivalent to that involved in executing a perfect corner shot. Length may not produce flashy shots that excite the spectators, but it does frustrate and exhaust your opponent by forcing him to try for shots beyond the level of his skill. It can even negate the shot-making ability of a champion. So think length!

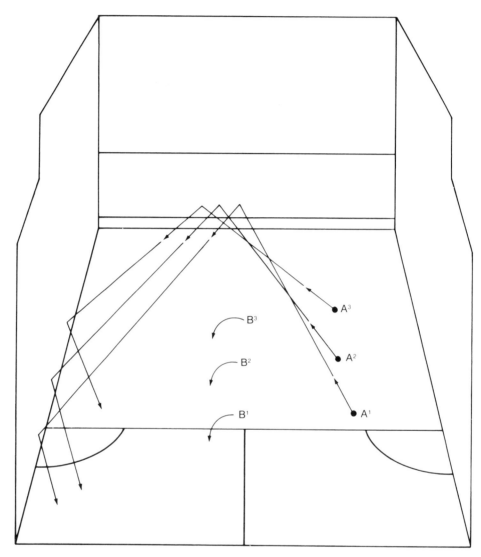

Figure 9.2. Length means not only the ability to have the ball die going to the back wall, but also the skill to direct the ball around your opponent. In all situations, B must turn and go back for the ball. Important: Make sure you hit the side wall with the ball before it goes to the floor.

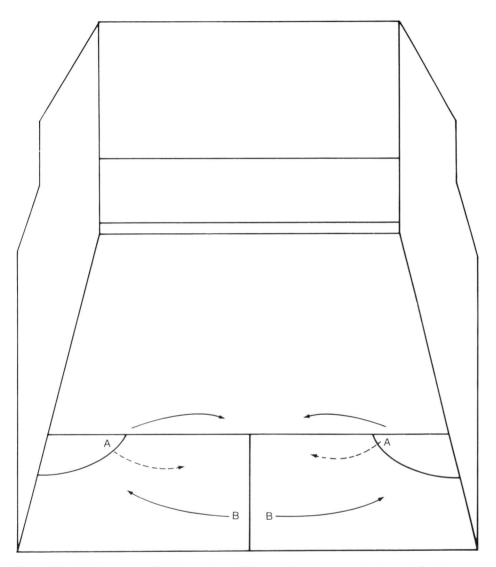

Figure 9.3.   A is the server; B is the receiver. This would be the general alignment for the server and receiver in the two situations above. It is best for server A always to serve with his forehand. Note: He should move to the T by going forward, not along the dotted lines. Receiver B should be facing toward nearest side wall when receiving.

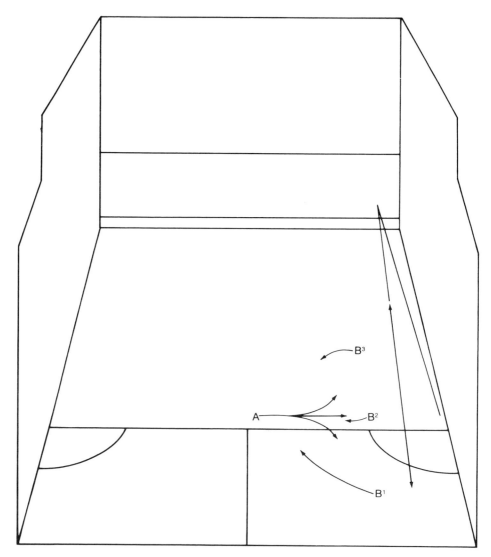

Figure 9.4.   A has free access to go for ball hit down the alley by B in situations B^1 and B^3. Note how B in these situations would move to take over T vacated by A. If B^2 were to hit down the alley, notice how he would impede A's path. Repeated infractions at B^2 would be cause for a let point (deliberate interference). B^2 can avoid this by hitting crosscourt.

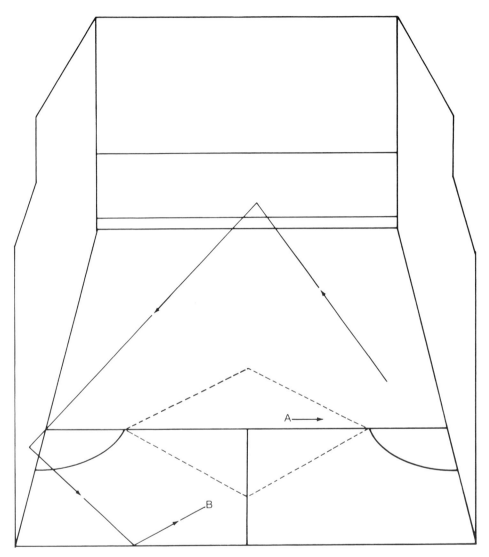

Figure 9.5. A has hit a poor shot or serve. B is thus in control of play even though he is not at the T. B in this situation can hit through diamond area, thus backing A out of position. Incidentally, it is always preferable to back the opponent rather than turn, because A has to give ground moving away from T (see Figure 9.6).

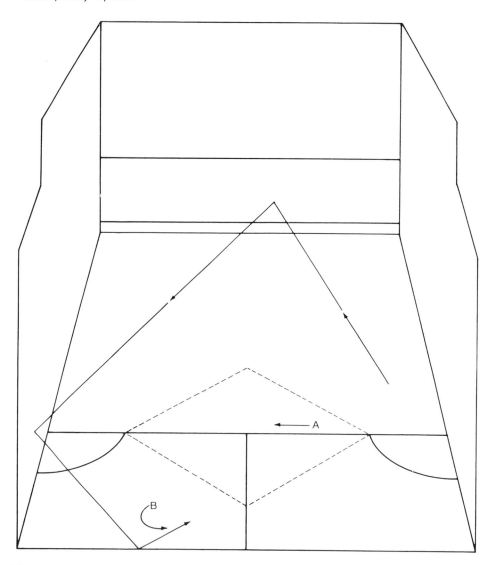

Figure 9.6.   Turning. In this situation, B has "turned on the ball." Note that A does not have to give as much ground. Only turn on the ball when necessary, when the ball is going fast around the court, or when you are caught off balance. Incidentally, the rule does not award striker the point if he hits his opponent with the ball in this situation.

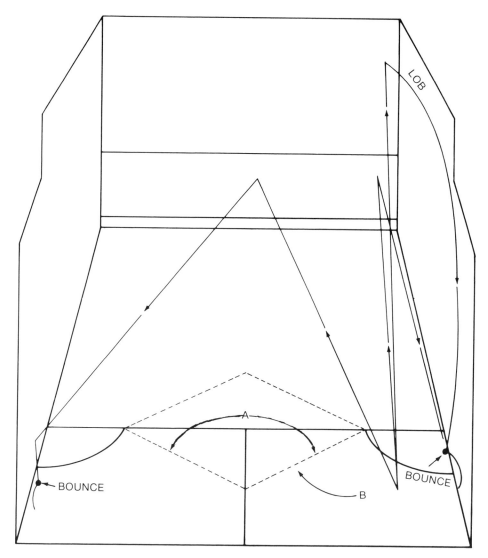

Figure 9.7. B should consider his position as defensive and play for length. If he were to hit hard and low, A is in great position to cut it off. B should hit for length to reverse the situation. His options are crosscourt or down the line as diagramed, to cause A to vacate T. The height of the ball above the telltale varies with B's power or A's ability to volley.

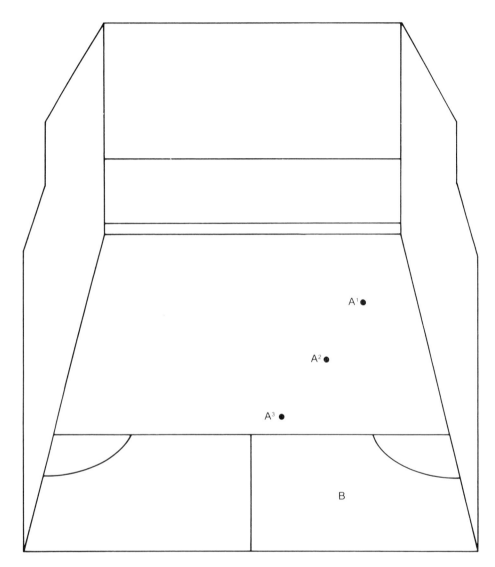

Figure 9.8. You must always be on guard and realize when you are overextended. In this situation, A at A¹ is overextended and should play crosscourt for length. At A², he is in a good situation, but should be on guard. Squash is not only a game of seeing but also of hearing. At A² he should pay attention to B's movements, either seen or heard. At A³, he is in a great situation to play all shots except a reverse corner. In all situations, A should hit forehand (right-handed play).

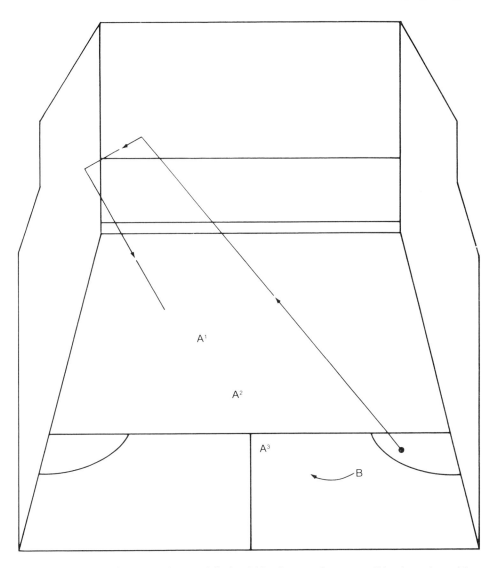

Figure 9.9. B has hit a poor shot, and A should back up as far as possible, through positions A^2 and A^3. Note how much more court A has to play the ball into if he moves back to A^3. Also note how far overextended he is if he plays the ball at A^1. At A^3, he must be careful to move forward as quickly as possible after he plays the shot so as to avoid a let situation.

10

Conditioning

All else being equal, physical condition may give a player the edge. Regardless of the level of play, the stamina to keep going beyond your opponent's limits is often the decisive advantage. Conditioning is also important as a preventive measure against the injuries that befall even champion players, so take time to warm up properly. Squash players seem more vulnerable to pulled muscles than players of other racquet games, probably because of the cool temperatures of most courts and the need to reach low for the ball.

Basic conditioning

Following are a few preliminary stretching exercises that can be performed on or off the court and are designed to increase limberness and prevent muscle injury. Combine them with the static method of stretching, in which you move slowly and rhythmically, holding a position at the first sign of discomfort. Do the following routine just before a game, and you'll enjoy the bonus of playing at your peak almost immediately.

Jumping jacks

Stand up, legs together, arms resting at your sides. Jump in place, simultaneously spreading the legs apart and raising the arms over your head. Repeat 20 to 30 times.

Purpose: Stimulates cardiovascular circulation and serves as an overall warm-up.

Toe touching

Stand up, knees straight, feet together, and bend forward from the waist slowly and carefully. Reach down until you feel the muscles in the back of your legs stretching. Hold this position for five to ten seconds and return to your standing position. Repeat 15 to 20 times.

Purpose: Stretches low back, hamstring, calf muscles, and flexes legs, calves, and back.

Wood chopping

Stand with legs apart and arms above the head. Keeping the elbows straight, bend forward freely as if you were chopping a piece of wood between your legs. Legs should be quite far apart for a good swing. Repeat 15 to 20 times.

Purpose: Activates the muscles used in raising the arms, as well as those on the front and back sides of the torso, and stretches muscles in the legs.

Squatting

Stand with heels close together with the weight of the body on the toes. Slowly squat down as far as possible, trying not to bend forward; then slowly rise again to the standing position. Repeat 10 to 20 times.

Purpose: Utilizes and stretches the flexors of the knee and the muscles of the calf and toes.

Additional stretching exercises

The preceding exercises are necessary, but elementary. For advanced training, these additional stretching exercises are recommended.

Figure 10.1. To stretch and flex lower back muscles, hip muscles, and abdominal muscles.

Figure 10.2. To increase flexibility in the calves and to stretch Achilles tendons.

Figure 10.3. To stretch hamstrings, calves, and lower back muscles.

Figure 10.4. To increase flexibility of the hips, spine, hamstrings, and back muscles; for added stretch and flexibility, spread legs further apart.

Figure 10.5. Variation of Figure 10.4 (purpose is the same); isolates each leg.

96

Figure 10.6. To stretch lower back muscles, muscles of the hamstring area, shoulders, and calves; to strengthen hip joint.

Figure 10.7. To flex the hip and knee joints fully; to stretch front hip muscles; to stretch groin muscles and muscles of the inside thigh.

Figure 10.8. Variation of Figure 10.7.

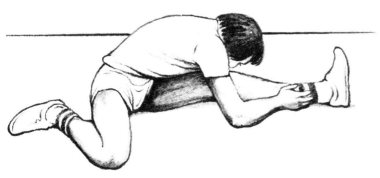

Figure 10.9. Extreme stretching of the knee and hip joints; to stretch back, shoulder, and hamstring muscles.

97

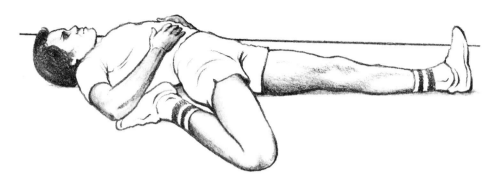

Figure 10.10. Extreme stretching of the knee and hip joints; to stretch front thigh muscles and the muscles of the front of the hip.

Figure 10.11. To stretch muscles of the back, the hamstrings, the chest, and the shoulders; to flex the spine.

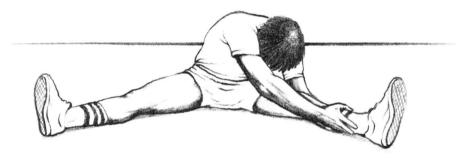

Figure 10.12. To stretch the back, shoulder, and hamstring muscles. Also to flex and stretch hip and groin muscles.

Figure 10.13. To stretch the back, shoulder, and hamstring muscles; stretching of the calf muscles is achieved by grasping the feet and pulling up.

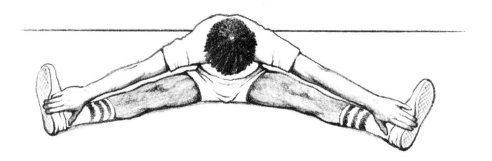

Figure 10.14. To stretch the muscles of the back and the front of the thigh; to stretch and strengthen muscles of the stomach, shoulders, and arms.

Figure 10.15. To stretch back and shoulder muscles and joints; to stretch hamstrings and calves.

Conditioning for championship play

Championship squash requires much more, because the strength, agility, and endurance demanded at that level increase yearly. Today's champions run distances, skip rope (excellent for balance, agility, and wrist action), and run agility drills in the court. Another innovation is weight training, a highly technical workout requiring expert personal supervision, which is generally done out of season. During preseason and off-season, or during any breaks in competition, top players also run about five miles at a pace slightly faster than a jog. If you intend to make distance running part of your routine, wear a good pair of special jogging shoes and run with your heel hitting the ground first, to prevent shin splints. Combine distance running with 100-yard sprints. Finally one of the most consistently useful exercises is hours of solo hitting in the court. Check yourself to be sure that you don't lose concentration and fall into sloppy stroking habits.

During the playing season, skipping rope and running sprints in the court are good ways of maintaining your performance. The following additional drills on the court can vary your practice routine and also help you chart physical progress. (Others are outlined in "Practice.") A good rule of thumb when exercising vigorously is "Strain without pain."

The penny drill

Place a penny in the six locations diagramed in Figure 10.16. Starting in a ready position at the T, sprint and pick up the pennies, returning to the T after each is picked up. Repeat as many times as you can; stay low, making sure to back up when you return to the T from the front wall.

Sprints in court

This drill is best done with two or more people in the court; when one is working out, the other can keep time.

Figure 10.16. The penny drill.

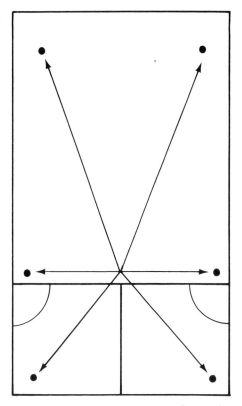

Your objective is to run as many times as you can from the back wall to the front wall, touching the floor each time while maintaining your pace. Change the leg you push off with each time you change direction. Count the number of times you touch the floor in one minute, then rest for a minute while you time your partner. As your conditioning progresses, increase the number of times you can sprint from one end of the court to the other and reduce the interval between rest periods. A benchmark: an athlete in average condition can do 18 laps in a minute and about five repetitions; someone nearing top condition can do 22 laps in a minute and up to 15 repetitions.

All players will increase their enjoyment and sense of accomplishment through physical conditioning. You will know that you are at or near the top of your form when you can push yourself without feeling exhausted.

11
Doubles

By now, my commitment to singles squash must be obvious to the reader, but I have to say that it cannot compare to the thrill of playing doubles. The synchronizing of two people in a joint effort is quite an achievement in itself, and when this challenge results in a winning effort, the shared rewards are multiple. Even if doubles squash did nothing more than extend the playing career of its participants, it would be a great game; yet it does still more, by enabling four people of unequal ability to play, compete, and have fun. Whereas tennis doubles require four participants of commensurate ability, this is not essential in squash. Nor is age as important in doubles squash as in singles. In 1976, for example, G. Diehl Mateer, Jr., partnered with his 19-year-old son, Gilbert, reached the finals of the U.S. National Doubles Championship. Such a feat would be impossible in tennis. The requirements of doubles squash are understanding of both the format of the game and the function of each player, and the ability to work with and complement your partner. In other words, a great singles player is not necessarily a great doubles player.

The following is intended to give you a start in doubles; the rest is up to you to discuss and work out with your partner. Most of you who look at doubles for the first time will probably think that it is the most confusing game in the world; everyone seems to be headed on a collision course. Well, that's not true. Collisions do happen, just as they do in singles, but once each person knows his role, collisions are rare. Crazy situations do arise and cause even longtime competitors playing in a championship to break up in laughter, but these serve only to demonstrate what a super enjoyable game doubles squash is.

As a general rule, successful doubles result when one partner supplies the power and the other the finesse. The power player's role is to force the opposition to the back of the court, thereby setting up the shot maker to use his touch in front. This is not an easy matter. Consequently it is important that the partners work together to create these openings. Players should cover the side of the court in which each is the most proficient and work in tandem with each other; they should not play one up and one back. Because the aim is to force the opponents to the back of the court, the most desirable position for you and your partner is approximately two feet in front of the service line. You want your opponent to be behind you and closer to the side wall.

Your approach to this position is the key to playing effective doubles. If your partner knows how you intend to get into position and where you are in any given situation, then he is free to concentrate on his man and his shot. The best way to get into a position in front of the man playing on your side of the court is to come up the middle. In this way, you maneuver your opponent toward the side wall without interfering with his shot. This move serves a number of functions: you can follow the play and ball easily and can move quickly to the shot; your opponent is likely to cause a let if he is not fast in getting out of the way; and your partner is able to see whether you are overextended and, if necessary, to move back and cover for you.

Probably no one has played the forehand court better than H. Hunter Lott, Jr. What made him a superstar was his power in combination with finesse, court sense, and determination to work hard to succeed. Some of Lott's forehand moves are diagramed in the pages that follow.

On the backhand, my selection as best player would be G. Diehl Mateer. Like Lott, Diehl had more than sheer skill. For example, although his singles forehand was more lethal than his singles backhand, in doubles his knowledge of position and his court sense made any backhand openings up front deadly to the opponents. Diehl's play on the backhand side is also shown in the accompanying diagrams.

Because squash doubles is played with the hard ball, you need a heavier racquet than for singles—one somewhere between nine and ten ounces. This extra weight is necessary not only because the ball is heavier but also because the court is larger (25 feet by 45 feet) and more high balls will come to you. Don't radically change your swing; just be prepared for these new variables. I think that you will compensate for the larger court automatically by lengthening your swing. And, whenever in doubt, play a let; in doubles squash, unlike singles, a let is played if you strike your opponent with the ball.

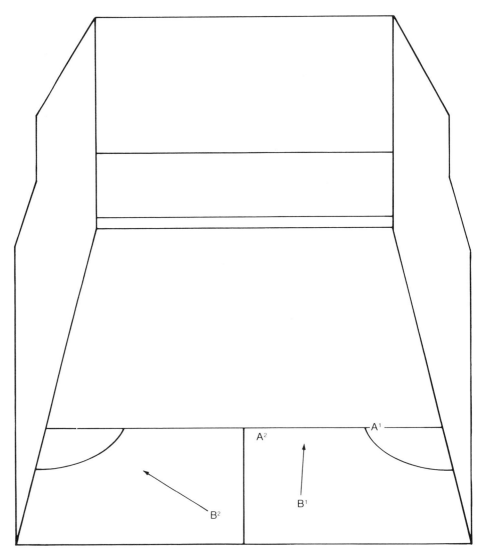

Figure 11.1. This is the generally accepted serving lineup for serving from the right court. Players A^1 and A^2 are partners. A^1 plays the right court and A^2 the left court. B^1 and B^2 do likewise.

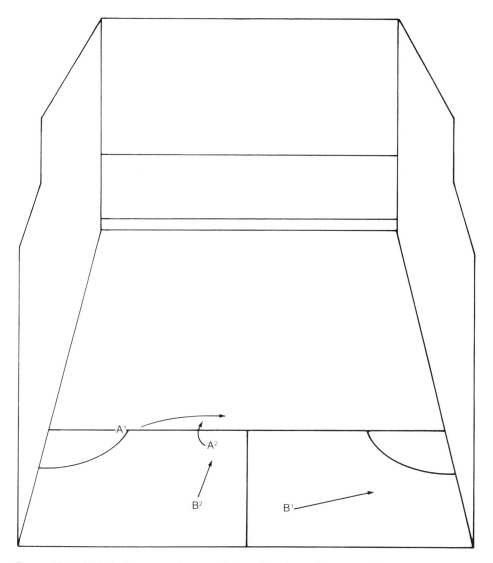

Figure 11.2. This is the generally accepted serving lineup from the left court. Note that A¹ crosses in front of partner A² in order to return to the right court, which he plays. The reverse would be true if A² were serving from the right court. Also, note that he moves well forward of the T position.

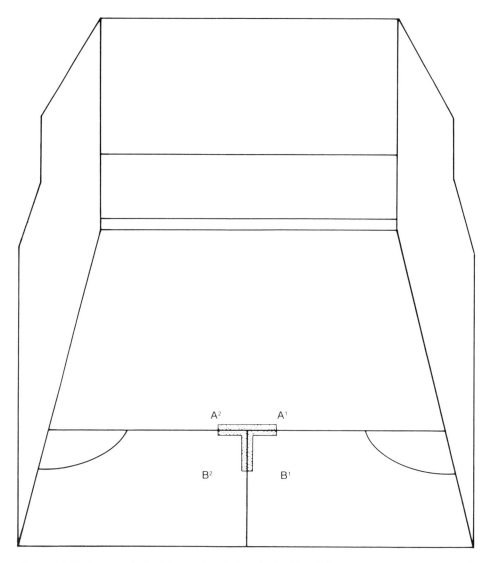

Figure 11.3. In squash doubles, just as in tennis doubles, it is best to play in tandem rather than one up and one back. It is interesting to note that the better teams play nearer to the middle of the court and try to force their opponents to play back and near to the side walls. Midcourt is a great volleying position.

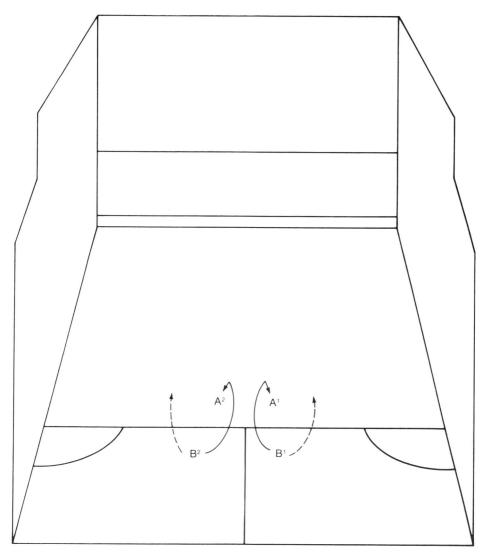

Figure 11.4. It is preferable for B¹ and B² to try to get into position by coming up the middle rather than the outside (dotted line) and then to back up if overextended (as shown).

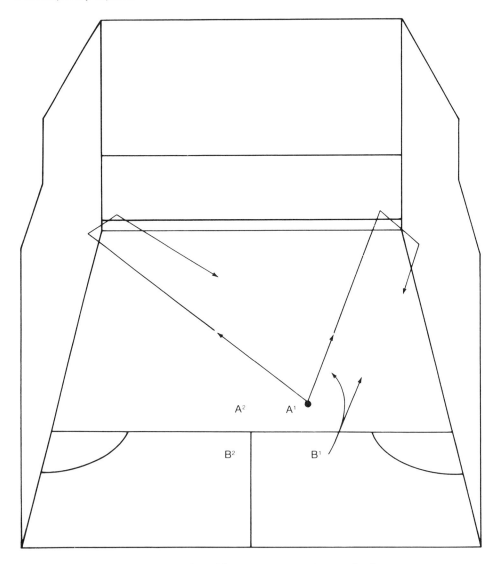

Figure 11.5.   B¹ must cover these shots. The reverse would be true for B².

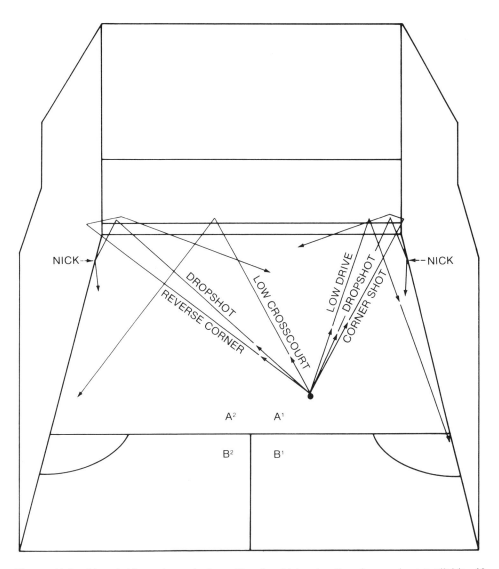

Figure 11.6. A¹ and A² are in perfect position for A¹ to play the six openings available. A² would have the same number of shots if he were playing the ball. Note how far B¹ and B² would have to go to retrieve these shots. Also note how A² is helping to shield A¹'s shots; this is his function. The same would be true if the situation were reversed.

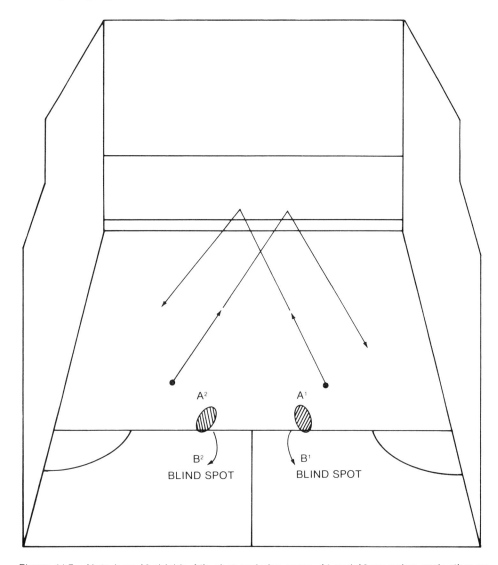

Figure 11.7. Note how A² shields A¹'s shot and vice versa. A¹ and A² are using each other as posts around which to hit the ball. It is important to remember that interference with vision is not cause for a let; however, you must not impede your opponent's access to the ball. Each partner is trying to create blind spots for his opponent.

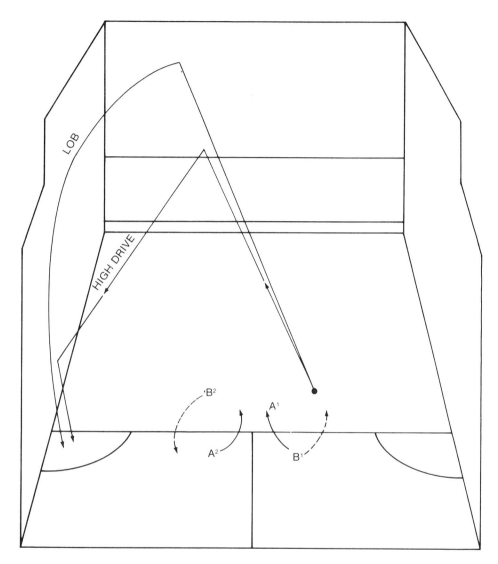

Figure 11.8.   A¹, with partner A² out of position, should hit either a lob over B² or a high drive that would break off the wall at shoulder height for B². B¹ must be moving up but alert, to cover for B². Note: If B¹ were to come up the outside (dotted line), he would be completely out of play and also might interfere with A¹'s swing.

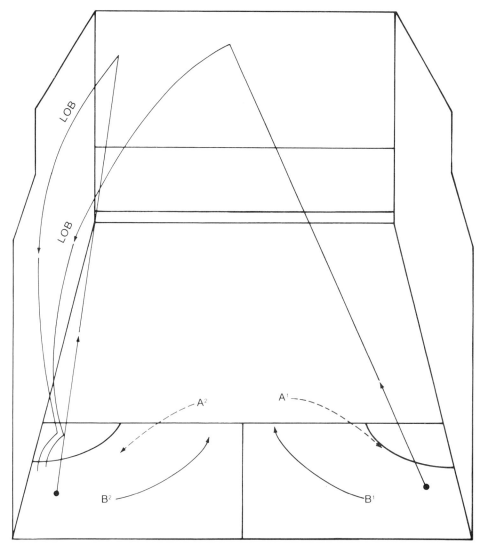

Figure 11.9. If either B¹ or B² is in the back court, it is best to lob, preferably down the line or crosscourt, to move A¹ and A² out of the middle.

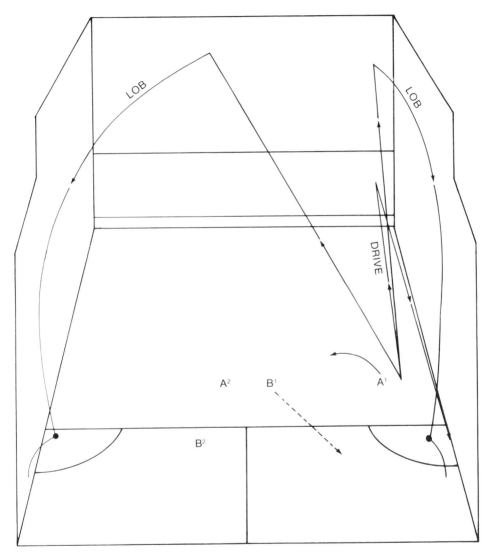

Figure 11.10.   In this situation, A¹ has only two replies on his side of the court, because B¹ has position on him. He should hit a high drive for length or a lob. If he is really in trouble, he should lob crosscourt to get help from his partner.

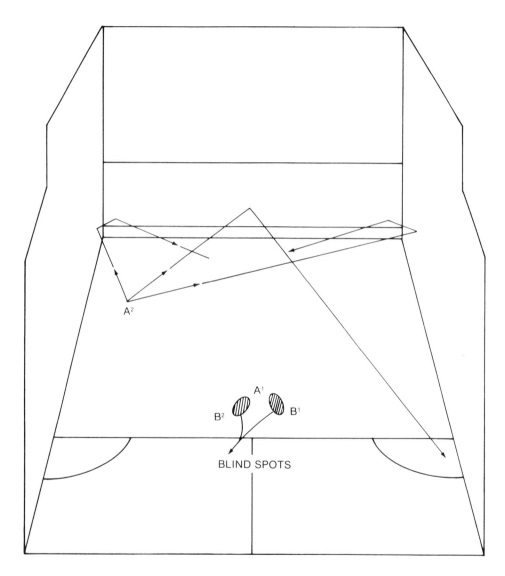

BLIND SPOTS

Figure 11.11. In this situation, when partner A² is drawn to the front of the court, A¹ also moves up at the middle. If A² is in trouble, he should lob to regain position control. However, if A² has a shot, then he should play it. Note the blind spots A¹ has created on B¹ and even on B².

Singles playing rules

1. Server

At the start of a match the choice to serve or receive shall be decided by the spin of a racquet. The server retains the serve until he loses a point, in which event he loses the serve.

2. Service

(a) The server, until the ball has left the racquet from the service, must stand with at least one foot on the floor within and not touching the line surrounding the service box and serve the ball onto the front wall above the service line and below the 16' line before it touches any other part of the court, so that on its rebound (return) it first strikes the floor within, but not touching, the lines of the opposite service court, either before or after touching any other wall or walls within the court. A ball so served is a good service, otherwise it is a Fault.

(b) If the first service is a Fault, the server shall serve again from the same side. If the server makes two consecutive Faults, he loses the point. A service called a Fault may not be played, but the receiver may volley any service which has struck the front wall in accordance with this rule.

(c) At the beginning of each game, and each time there is a new server, the ball shall be served by the winner of the previous point from whichever service box the server elects and thereafter alternately until the service is lost or until the end of the game. If the server serves from the wrong box there shall be no penalty and the service shall count as if served from the correct box, provided, however, that if the receiver does not attempt to return the service, he may demand that it be served from the other box, or if, before the receiver attempts to return the service, the Referee calls a Let (See Rule 9), the service shall be made from the other box.

(d) A ball is in play from the moment at which it is delivered in service until (1) the point is decided; (2) a Fault, as defined in 2(a) is made; or (3) a Let or Let Point occurs (See Rules 9 and 10).

3. Return of service and subsequent play

(a) A return is deemed to be made at the instant the ball touches the racquet of the player making the return. To make a good return of a service or of a subsequent return the ball must be struck on the volley or before it has touched the floor twice, and reach the front wall on the fly above the tell-tale and below the 16′ line, and it may touch any wall or walls within the court before or after reaching the front wall. On any return the ball may be struck only once. It may not be "carried" or "double-hit."

(b) If the receiver fails to make a good return of a good service, the server wins the point. If the receiver makes a good return of service, the players shall alternate making returns until one player fails to make a good return. The player failing to make a good return loses the point.

(c) Until the ball has been touched or has hit the floor twice, it may be struck at any number of times.

(d) If at any time after a service the ball hits outside the playing surfaces of the court (the ceiling and/or lights, or on or above a line marking the perimeters of the playing surfaces of the court), the player so hitting the ball loses the point, unless a Let or a Let Point occurs. (See Rules 9 and 10.)

4. Score

Each point won by a player shall add one to his score.

5. Game

The player who first scores fifteen points wins the game excepting that:

(a) At "thirteen all" the player who has first reached the score of thirteen must elect one of the following before the next serve:

    (1) Set to five points—making the game eighteen points.

    (2) Set to three points—making the game sixteen points.

    (3) No set, in which event the game remains fifteen points.

(b) At "fourteen all" provided the score has not been "thirteen all" the player who has first reached the score of fourteen must elect one of the following before the next serve:

    (1) Set to three points—making the game seventeen points.

    (2) No set, in which event the game remains fifteen points.

6. Match

The player who first wins three games wins the match, except that a player may be awarded the match at any time upon the retirement, default or disqualification of an opponent.

7. Right to play ball

Immediately after striking the ball a player must get out of an opponent's way and must:

(a) Give an opponent a fair view of the ball, provided, however, interference purely with an opponent's vision in following the flight of the ball is not a Let (See Rule 9).

(b) Give an opponent a fair opportunity to get to and/or strike at the ball in and from any position on the court elected by the opponent; and

(c) Allow an opponent to play the ball to any part of the front wall or to either side wall near the front wall.

8. Ball in play touching player

(a) If a ball in play, after hitting the front wall, but before being returned again, shall touch either player, or anything he wears or carries (other than the racquet of the player who makes the return) the player so touched loses the point, except as provided in Rule 9(a) or 9(b).

(b) If a ball in play touches the player who last returned it or anything he wears or carries before it hits the front wall, the player so touched loses the point.

(c) If a ball in play, after being struck by a player on a return, hits the player's opponent or anything the opponent wears or carries before reaching the front wall:

   (1) The player who made the return shall lose the point if the return would not have been good.

   (2) The player who made the return shall win the point if the ball, except for such interference,

would have hit the front wall fairly; provided, however, the point shall be a Let (see Rule 9) if:

(i) The ball would have touched some other wall before so hitting the front wall.

(ii) The ball has hit some other wall before hitting the player's opponent or anything he wears or carries.

(iii) The player who made the return shall have turned following the ball around prior to playing the ball.

(d) If a player strikes at and misses the ball, he may make further attempts to return it. If, after being missed, the ball touches his opponent or anything he wears or carries:

(1) If the player might otherwise have made a good return, the point shall be a Let.

(2) If the player could not have made a good return, he shall lose the point.

If any further attempt is successful but the ball, before reaching the front wall, touches his opponent or anything he wears or carries and Rule 8(c)(2) applies, the point shall be a Let.

(e) When there is no referee, if the player who made the return does not concede that the return would not have been good, or alternatively, the player's opponent does not concede that the ball has hit him (or anything he wears or carries) and would have gone directly to the front wall without first touching any other wall, the point shall be a Let.

(f) When there is no referee, if the players are unable to agree whether 8(d)(1) or 8(d)(2) applies, the point shall be a Let.

9. Let

A let is the playing over of a point.

On the replay of the point the server (1) is entitled to two serves even if a Fault was called on the original point,

(2) must serve from the correct box even if he served from the wrong box on the original point, and (3) provided he is a new server, may serve from a service box other than the one selected on the original point.

In addition to the Lets described in Rules 2(c) and 8(c)(3), the following are Lets if the player whose turn it is to strike the ball could otherwise have made a good return:

(a) When such player's opponent violates Rule 7.

(b) When owing to the position of such player, his opponent is unable to avoid being touched by the ball.

(c) When such player refrains from striking at the ball because of a reasonable fear of injuring his opponent.

(d) When such player before or during the act of striking or striking at the ball is touched by his opponent, his racquet or anything he wears or carries.

(e) When on the first bounce from the floor the ball hits on or above the six and one half foot line on the back wall; and

(f) When a ball in play breaks. If a player thinks the ball has broken while play is in progress he must nevertheless complete the point and then immediately request a Let, giving the ball to the Referee for inspection. The Referee shall allow a Let only upon such immediate request if the ball in fact proves to be broken (See Rule 13(c)).

A player may request a Let or a Let Point (See Rule 10). A request by a player for a Let shall automatically include a request for a Let Point. Upon such request, the Referee shall allow a Let, Let Point or no Let.

No Let shall be allowed on any stroke a player makes unless he requests such before or during the act of striking or striking at the Ball.

The Referee may not call or allow a Let as defined in this Rule 9 unless such Let is requested by a player; provided, however, the Referee may call a Let at any time (1) when there is interference with play caused by any factor beyond the control of the players, or (2) when he fears that a player is about to suffer severe physical injury.

10. Let Point

A Let Point is the awarding of a point to a player when an opponent unnecessarily violates Rule 7(b) or 7(c).

An unnecessary violation occurs (1) when the player fails to make the necessary effort within the scope of his normal ability to avoid the violation, thereby depriving his opponent of a clear opportunity to attempt a winning shot, or (2) when the player has repeatedly failed to make the necessary effort within the scope of his normal ability to avoid such violations.

The Referee may not award a Let Point as defined in this Rule 10 unless such Let Point or a Let (see Rule 9) is requested by a player.

When there is no referee, if a player does not concede that he has unnecessarily violated Rule 7(b) or 7(c), the point shall be a Let.

11. Continuity of Play

Play shall be continuous from the first service of each game until the game is concluded. Play shall never be suspended solely to allow a player to recover his strength or wind. The provisions of the Rule 11 shall be strictly construed. The Referee shall be the sole judge of intentional delay, and, after giving due warning, he must default the offender.

Between each game play may be suspended by either player for a period not to exceed two minutes. Between the third and fourth games play may be suspended by either player for a period not to exceed five minutes. Except during the five minute period at the end of the third game, no player may leave the court without permission of the referee.

Except as otherwise specified in this Rule 11, the Referee may suspend play for such reason and for such period of time as he may consider necessary.

If play is suspended by the Referee because of injury to one of the players, such player must resume play within one hour from the point and game score existing at the time play was suspended or default the match, provided, however, if a player suffers cramps or pulled muscles, play may be suspended by the Referee once during a match for such player for a period not to exceed five minutes after which time such player must resume play or default the match.

In the event the Referee suspends play other than for injury to a player, play shall be resumed when the Referee determines the cause of such suspension of play has been eliminated, provided, however, if such cause of delay cannot be rectified within one hour, the match shall be postponed to such time as the Tournament Committee determines. Any such suspended match shall be resumed from the point and game score existing at the time the match was stopped unless the Referee and both players unanimously agree to play the entire match or any part of it over.

12. Attire and equipment

(a) The color of a player's shirt or trousers may be either white or a solid pastel. The Referee's decision as to a player's attire shall be final.

(b) A standard singles ball as specified in the Court, Racquet and Ball Specifications of this Association shall be used.

(c) A racquet as specified in the Court, Racquet and Ball Specifications of this Association shall be used.

13. Condition of ball

(a) No ball, before or during a match, may be artifically treated, that is, heated or chilled.

(b) At any time, when not in the actual play of a point, another ball may be substituted by the mutual consent of the players or by decision of the Referee.

(c) A ball shall be determined broken when it has a

crack which extends through both its inner and outer surfaces. The ball may be squeezed only enough to determine
the extent of the crack. A broken ball shall be replaced and
the preceding point shall be a Let (See Rule 9(f)).

(d) A cracked (but not broken) ball may be replaced by
the mutual consent of the players or by decision of the
Referee, and the preceding point shall stand.

14. Court

(a) The singles court shall be as specified in the Court,
Racquet and Ball Specifications of this Association.

(b) No equipment of any sort shall be permitted to
remain in the court during a match other than the ball used
in play, the racquets being used by the players, and the
clothes worn by them. All other equipment, such as extra
balls, extra racquets, sweaters when not being worn, towels,
bathrobes, etc., must be left outside the court. A player who
requires a towel or cloth to wipe himself or anything he
wears or carries should keep same in his pocket or securely
fastened to his belt or waist.

15. Referee

(a) A Referee shall control the game. This control shall
be exercised from time the players enter the court. The
Referee may limit the time of the warm up period to five
minutes, or shall terminate a longer warm up period so that
the match commences at the scheduled time.

(b) The Referee's decision on all questions of play shall
be final except as provided in Rule 15(c).

(c) Two judges may be appointed to act on any appeal
by a player to a decision of the Referee. When such judges
are acting in a match, a player may appeal any decision of
the Referee to the judges, except a decision under Rules 11,
12(a), 13, 15(a) and 15(f). If one judge agrees with the

Referee, the Referee's decision stands; if both judges disagree with the Referee, the judges' decision is final. The judges shall make no ruling unless an appeal has been made. The decision of the judges shall be announced promptly by the Referee.

(d) A player may not request the removal or replacement of the Referee or a judge during a match.

(e) A player shall not state his reason for his request under Rule 9 for a Let or Let Point or for his appeal from any decision of the Referee provided, however, that the Referee may request the player to state his reasons.

(f) A Referee serving without judges, after giving due warning of the penalty of this Rule 15(f), in his descretion may disqualify a player for speech or conduct unbecoming to the game of squash racquets, provided that a player may be disqualified without warning if, in the opinion of such referee, he has deliberately caused physical injury to his oponent.

When two judges are acting in a match, the Referee in his discretion, upon the agreement of both judges, may disqualify a player with or without prior warning for speech or conduct unbecoming to the game of squash racquets.

Glossary

Ace—a shot that one's opponent cannot touch with his racquet.

Alley or rail shot—a shot played parallel and close to a side wall. *See* **Down-the-line shot.**

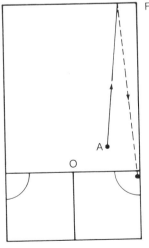

Figure G.1. Alley or rail.

Angle shot—a shot striking the side wall on its way to the front wall.

Appeal—a request by a player to the **Referee** to reconsider a call.

Backing on the ball—backing up to take a ball that has broken out into the middle of the court.

Back swing—the windup for a stroke.

Back-wall shot—a shot taken off the back wall before it hits the floor for a second time.

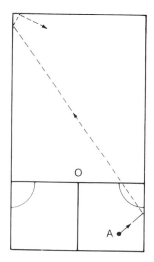
Figure G.2. Boast.

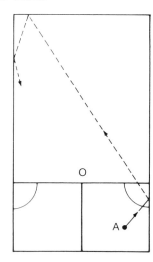
Figure G.3. Boast for nick.

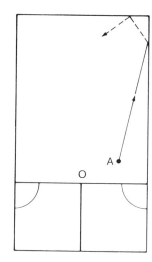
Figure G.4. Corner.

Boast—a return made by using the side wall, normally played from the back of the court.

Boast for nick—same as a **Boast,** except that player is definitely in a position to make an attack.

Coming around—when a player calls "Turning" or "Around" to warn his opponent that he is turning to take a ball breaking off the side and back walls.

Corner shot— similar to **Angle shot** but played close to the front wall.

Covering a shot—placing oneself in a position to block an opponent from making a shot; an illegal move.

Crosscourt—playing a ball to the opposite side of the court.

Die—when the ball fails to bounce.

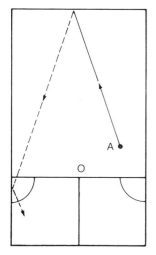

Figure G.5.
Crosscourt or V.

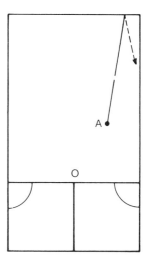

Figure G.6.
Dropshot.

Doubles—squash played by four people (two on a side) in a court 45 feet by 25 feet—as opposed to 32 feet by 18½ feet for singles—using a heavier ball.

Down-the-line shot—same as **Alley shot.**

Drive—a ball hit hard after the bounce.

Dropshot—a ball hit softly so that its second bounce falls close to the front wall.

Fault—an incorrect serve.

Follow-through—continuation of swing after ball has been struck.

Foot fault—a fault caused by the server's not having at least one foot grounded and wholly within **Service box.**

Frame—unstrung racquet.

Gallery—spectator's area.

Game—part of a match.

Get—return of a difficult shot.

Good length—describes a ball that is so deep that the opponent has trouble deciding whether to play it before or after it hits the back wall. Creates a difficult shot in either case.

Half volley—a ball hit immediately after the bounce.

Hand in—a term generally used in **Doubles** to signify the serving team.

Hand out—the term signifying the receiving team in **Doubles.**

Judge—one of two officials who aid the **Referee** in making decisions.

Let—a point that must be replayed.

Let point—a point awarded to a player because of his opponent's deliberate illegal interference. *See* "Rules."

Lob—a ball lofted high on the front wall.

Marker—scorekeeper.

Match—usually best three out of five games.

Monkey doubles—**Doubles** played in a singles court with a singles ball, using racquets with handles that have been cut down.

Nick—a ball that hits the junction of the floor and side wall, or the floor and back wall, rolls out, and is impossible to return.

No let—**Referee's** decision to refuse a player's request for a **Let**.

No set—call made optionally by the receiver at 13-all or 14-all (in both cases the game is 15).

Philadelphia shot or Philadelphia boast—a reverse boast; a trick shot.

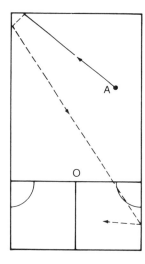

Figure G.7.
Philadelphia boast.

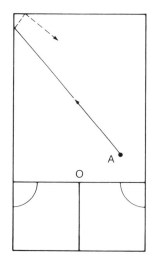

Figure G.8.
Reverse corner.

Put-away—a shot that cannot be retrieved.

Quarter circle—area in which the server places one foot while serving. *See* **Service box.**

Rail shot—same as the **Alley shot.**

Rally—a series of shots.

Referee—the official who controls the game.

Reverse corner—a **Corner shot** hit from the opposite side of the court.

Service box—same as **Quarter circle.**

T—the strategic center of the court, where the service line and center service line form a T.

Telltale—the 17-inch-high rectangle of sheet metal at the bottom of the front wall that gives off a ringing sound when struck by the ball. The ball must clear it in order to be good.

Tin—slang for **Telltale.**

Touch—a player's finesse in hitting **Corner shots** and **Drop shots.**

Turning on ball—same as **Coming around.**

Volley—ball hit before it touches the floor.

Winner—same as **Put-away.**

Index